CW01662346

Usually when we trace the line of offspring ou[t]
it is the men who take center stage. But in this b
weaves the story of the Bible through the line c
with simplicity and insight.

– Nancy Guthrie, Bible teacher and author of *Even Better Than Eden*

It's beautifully rich. It's theologically deep. It's a book that will help your heart to sing, as you see God's character, his faithfulness and ultimately the Lord Jesus Christ unveiled, at the centre of women's lives through the Bible. Read it, savour it and let Nana's words enrich and deepen your understanding of God's plan for all of history!

– Sarah Dargue, podcast host and author of *Bumps, Babies and the Gospel*

We know that the story of the gospel climaxes with the birth of the man, Jesus Christ. What is forgotten is that this narrative not only involved women but is often told by women. To ignore their voice is to neglect significant storytellers of the history of redemption. *The Seed of the Woman* preserves this tradition. Not only does it portray the gospel with beauty and grace, but it also reminds us that the Lord used heroic and faithful women to give birth to messianic hope, tend to its care, preserve that story, and share it with others.

– Peter Y. Lee, Professor of Old Testament, Reformed Theological Seminary, Washington, DC

All women hold within themselves the beauty and dignity of their Creator, because they are made in His image. We can't see God, but we can know about Him through His creation, women included. But it is through the specific women in the Old Testament that we can see the shape and substance of our Savior coming into focus. Though flawed and often misguided, they point ahead to Jesus and help us understand (and long for) His necessary life, death, and resurrection. That's why I'm so grateful for Nana Dolce and her beautifully descriptive reflections on the women of the Old Testament. These women and their stories set our hearts ablaze for Christ.

– Christine Hoover, author of *Seek First the Kingdom* and *How to Thrive as a Pastor's Wife*

Nana Dolce's book isn't another character study of women of the Bible – she knows we need more than finding a woman in our Scriptures. Instead, she uniquely reveals how the stories of the known and not-so-known women lead us to the bigger story of Jesus Christ ... and she does it well. Her writing made the stories come alive, and my heart delighted in the kindness and grace of God.

– Taylor Turkington, Bible teacher and director of BibleEquipping

Nana Dolce has taken great care to present the stories of the women who played significant roles in the plan of redemption. The light she sheds on these often overlooked women is long overdue. The methodological approach is far beyond devotional. It is faithful biblical exposition with gospel-centered reflections. Her warm and pleasant spirit comes across the pages of this work. Readers will appreciate the well-written, easily read, and thought-provoking narratives of these amazing women.

– Patrick J. Walker, Senior Pastor, The New Macedonia Baptist Church, Washington, DC

NANA DOLCE

the SEED *of the* WOMAN

30 narratives that point to Jesus

First published in Great Britain in 2022

British Cataloguing in Publication Data
A record for this book is available from the British Library

ISBN: 978-1-78397-330-9

Designed by Jude May
Cover image © Yayasya | iStock

Printed in Denmark

Evangelical Press (EP Books), an imprint of 10Publishing
Unit C, Tomlinson Road, Leyland, PR25 2DY, England
Email: epbooks@10ofthose.com
Website: www.epbooks.org

3 5 7 10 8 6 4 2

Contents

Foreword

In her opening chapter, Nana Dolce draws our attention to the Bible's first poem (Gen 1:27), the one that marvels at the wonderful and mysterious notion that humanity is made "in the image of God." After all the divine work of creation in this chapter, this poem represents the pinnacle of the account leaving the biblical author simply overwhelmed with the "very-goodness" of it all. Some ideas are so wonderful, only a poem will do.

We talk a lot today about the dignity, beauty, and honor of humanity as *imago Dei*, but the true universality of the "image of God" is often lost in discussions about the women of the Bible. Women play a crucial role in the development of the Old Testament story, serving as the linchpins for so many of the events in redemptive history. I think of the creation of Eve in Genesis 2, Miriam's song in Exodus 15, Deborah and Jael in Judges 4 – 5, Hannah in 1 Samuel 1 – 2, and Abigail in 1 Samuel 25, just to name a few. In each case, the female protagonist is presented, speaks, and acts in ways that might surprise us and even challenge our unexamined beliefs about what it means to be a man or woman in the service of God.

These stories about powerful women can remind us of how we as readers bring so much of our own cultural commitments (whether conservative, progressive, or other) to the act of biblical interpretation. As a result, we do well to allow ourselves and our cultural context to be interrogated by the Word of God, always praying with the psalmist, "Search me, O God, and know my heart … see if there be any grievous way in me, and lead me in the way everlasting" (Ps. 139:23–24). Be encouraged that this is exactly the kind of prayer that our loving Father is pleased to answer.

What is so profound about the book that you are holding in your hands is the direction that Dolce chooses to take with these biblical passages featuring women. She does not shy away from the difficult questions, but she is not constrained by them either. Rather, she takes the teaching about the image of God in Genesis 1 seriously and asks what the women in these stories tell us about the character of the God in whose image they are made. More specifically, she asks what their stories tell us about his Son, the full embodiment of the Godhead (Col. 2:9). As she explores these questions, she artfully develops her argument that the Old Testament is truly the pre-announcement of the gospel of Jesus Christ.

You are in the hands of an able teacher, and I commend this study to any true student of the whole counsel of God. As you follow her discussion, attune your ear to the voice of the Shepherd speaking to you through the lives of these biblical women.

Scott Redd

President & Stephen B. Elmer Professor of Old Testament
Reformed Theological Seminary, Washington, DC

Introduction

Why Old Testament women and Christ?

Jesus offered a sermon to two disheartened disciples in Luke 24. They presumed the Lord dead as they trudged along a road toward Emmaus. The risen Christ met them on that road and opened the Scriptures to them. These unseeing disciples had failed to perceive his coming suffering and glory in the Old Testament Scriptures. So *"beginning with Moses and all the Prophets, he interpreted to them in all the Scriptures the things concerning himself"* (Lk. 24:27). According to Jesus, all of the Old Testament was written to point to him.

The words of Old Testament Scripture are not merely the tales of the godly and godless, but a pre-announcement of Christ's work in salvation. But does this include the narratives of Old Testament women as well? How do the stories of these women fit into the redemptive drama that culminates in Christ? Do women like Leah, Jael, and Abigail *also* point us to Jesus? This book shouts a resounding "yes"!

In *The Seed of the Woman*, we tell the story of the Old Testament through the narratives of women. Our goal is to follow the developing theme of the "promised Seed" across Old Testament history. We divide our journey into six periods of redemptive history: (1) Creation and the Fall, (2) Women of Genesis, (3) Women of the Exodus, (4) Women of the conquest and the time of the judges, (5) Women from Israel's monarchy to the Exile, and (6) Women Between the Testaments to Christ.

Our chapters take us from Genesis to Jesus in the New Testament. We examine the narratives of thirty women along the way to find Christ, the promised Seed of the Woman (Gen. 3:15).

Why biblical theology?

The Bible is one book. Its forty different authors are inspired by one divine author. It was written on one subject: God's redemption of sinners through the person and work of Christ. Jesus is the interpretive center of the Scriptures and biblical theology helps us to see that. It takes us historically and chronologically across the pages of Scripture to reveal the "big picture" of God's work through his Son. This book isn't a mere "recap" of Bible stories but an intentional tracing of a progressive theme across Scripture. In other words, we follow a thread in the fabric of the story of redemption as it unfolds to display Jesus.

Women are part of that grand story. So, we study their narratives, not just as inspirations for faithful living, but to see God's work in salvation history. Like the disciples of Emmaus, we want our hearts to burn as we recognize our Christ at the center of the big story that governs all human history – and who is also our hope for today (Lk. 24:32).

Good news that proves true

Readers of this book live in a post-Genesis 3 world. We are women with full hands, we battle noisy distractions, and face cunning temptations. We need books that preach Christ. We need the good news that proves true – not false promises that glitter then fade. *The Seed of the Woman* is a book on women that is ultimately about a Man. It's written to show Christ as the interpretive center of the Old Testament Scriptures. Each chapter begins with a reflection point – this isn't a chapter summary but a statement on God's character for your meditation. The back flap contains a visual timeline of Old Testament history which shows the historical placement of the women featured in this book, helping you to see the big picture of Old Testament history and where these women in the Bible appear. As you consider their lives, I pray that you will recognize yourself as a woman whose life is also meant to point to Jesus within the unfolding drama of the biggest story ever told!

PART ONE:

Creation, Fall, the Promised Seed, and Eve

1

Creation

The Bible's first poem

(Genesis 1 – 2)

Reflection

The God who acts alone in Genesis 1 is also the covenant Lord God who initiates relationship with his created beings in Genesis 2. God's plan from creation was to dwell with his people.

This book on women begins with God. In fact, as you read, you'll notice that we never really turn our attention away from him. He is at the center of every chapter. After all, the Bible isn't primarily about women (or men) – but about the God who creates women and men and who redeems them through his Son.[1] This God and his Son are our focal point as we journey across Scripture. We start in Genesis with the ancient story of creation, retold with a focus on poetry.

I'm no poet, but motherhood has made me a reciter of rhymes. Most Dr.-Seuss-loving mommas will tell you that poetry can convey new ideas to children more vividly than literal prose. A well-composed rhyme is a powerful teaching tool. Perhaps that's why poetry fills the Bible from Genesis to Revelation (and shows up so early on in Scripture). God's creative work in Genesis 1 is ordered in a sequential flow that some would argue as poetic. But in Genesis 1:27, we read a line that appears to be a true poem. The verse has much to say about God and the people he makes.

Context for this poem begins in Genesis 1:1: *"In the beginning, God created the heavens and the earth."* Moses is considered the author of these words (and the first five books of the Bible). He wrote to an unsteady nation of formerly enslaved people who were learning to trust God as his own possession (Ex. 6:7). This introductory sentence of Scripture is key to the story Moses tells. It reminds Israel, and us, of God's supremacy. The world isn't the result of chance but *his* direct and creative work. Moses refers to God as *Elohim* (the mighty One) throughout Genesis 1.[2] And indeed, here we meet a mighty God who commands a void nothing into a vivid something.

God is the only speaker and actor in Genesis 1. And this shouldn't surprise us – after all, he alone is self-existent and eternal. Like a designer – more masterful than Chip and Joanna Gaines – he used words to build three distinct settings in the first three days of creation. First, he made day and night, then sky and sea, and finally, dry land and vegetation (Gen. 1:2–13). In the following three days, he progressively filled each space with a matching creature: cosmological lights, birds and marine life, land animals and people – the crown of his creation (Gen. 1:14–26).

Our author shares all this with us in an orderly account. But when he gets to the making of humankind, he parts from prose into poetry. And here we have, what might be, the Bible's first poem. Genesis 1:27 is a verse that celebrates the hallmark of God's creation: the man and the woman.

So God created man in his own image,
in the image of God he created him;
male and female he created them.

The word "created" seems to serve as the refrain to Moses' song here. He repeats it three times. The poem appears to shout along with Genesis 2, "Yes!" It was *God* who *created* humankind! *He* took dust from the ground. He turned, formed, and molded it into a man (the word for "Man" is *Adam* in Hebrew). It was *he* who breathed life into Adam's nostrils. The man became a living creature because God *created* him (Gen. 2:7).

And God – seeing that it wasn't good for Adam to be alone (Gen. 2:18) – took his rib and fashioned a woman (she's named Eve later in the story). Man and Woman are created beings. Male and female God *created* them (Gen. 1:27). Scripture's first poem emphasizes God's preeminence as Creator and humanity as creature. But the verse has a second emphasis – here, a majestic God forms dusty people in his own likeness.

I have the joy of parenting daughters who resemble their mother. My eldest has been called her momma's "twin." She's a mini version of me with the same thick curly hair and broad smile. She looks like me and yet Someone far greater has placed his image on her. Human beings carry the distinction of the *imago Dei* (the image of God). We were created to be replicas and vice-regents of God – creatures formed with the unique capacity to reflect God's holy character in our rule and care for the world.[3] And this is true of every human being, from the smallest embryo to the oldest amongst us. No age, ethnic, or social group bears more of God's likeness than another. Every human being is made to mirror God – and it starts at creation.

God blessed the first couple and commanded them to *"Be fruitful and multiply and fill the earth and subdue it"* (Gen. 1:28). Like God, these two were to order and stock the earth. God planted a garden in Eden and placed Adam there to work and keep it (Gen. 2:8–15). He provided everything the man and woman needed to obey his creation, filling, and ruling mandates. They had marriage, work, abundant food, and something beyond our imagination – God's visible presence.

The author seems to highlight this visible presence with the introduction of a new name for God in Genesis 2. He calls him *Yahweh Elohim* ("the LORD God," Gen. 2:4). This is the personal and covenant name of God. The transcendent God who acts alone in Genesis 1 is also the omnipresent personal Lord God who initiates relationship with his created beings in Genesis 2. The Bible begins with a Creator who abides with his creation and will end with a God who dwells with his people in a new creation (Rev. 21:3). In between is a drama in which Woman plays a tragic key role. And yet, as we will see, the mercy of *Yahweh Elohim* will read like poetry in motion in this story of Scripture.

2

The Fall and the Seed

The Fall of mankind and the Seed of woman

(Genesis 3)

Reflection

God judged Woman and Adam – but not without mercy. He covered the depraved woman and inserted her into this glorious drama of redemption.

The Bible introduces human speech with a serenade to Woman. Adam's Genesis 2:23 song to his bride are his only words recorded before the Fall. Man was created first, but Woman wasn't received as an inferior second. On the contrary, she was welcomed as the complementary gift that canceled God's "not good" pronouncement of Genesis 2:18. The union of Adam and Woman completed God's work of creation on the sixth day. Genesis 2 closes with the pair together, naked, and not ashamed (Gen. 2:25).

The next chapter opens in the same glorious setting: God's Garden in Eden. But the splendor of Genesis 1 and 2 is followed by the treachery of Genesis 3. God had provided bountifully for the first couple. His words to Adam were these: *"You may surely eat of every tree of the garden, but of the tree of the knowledge of good and evil you shall not eat, for in the day that you eat of it you shall surely die"* (Gen. 2:16–17). Presumably, Woman knew these words. Yet soon after the chapter begins, we find her in conversation with a talking snake – and the topic is snack time.

Like a sneaky gossip fishing for news, the serpent probed, twisting God's command from generous to stingy: *"Did God actually say, 'You shall not eat of any tree in the garden'"* (Gen. 3:1)? The exact opposite was true, the couple could eat of *every* tree – but one. Woman's answer (or perhaps Adam's intercession) should have crushed this lie with swift truth. Instead, Woman's first recorded words in Scripture alter God's command by adding a prohibition never given: *"We may eat of the fruit of the trees in the garden, but God said, 'You shall not eat of the fruit of the tree that is in the midst of the garden, neither shall you touch it, lest you die'"* (Gen. 3:2–3).

The animal that the couple had been created to rule was now schooling Woman – and questioning God. The serpent wasted no time in casting doubts on God's motives. *"You will not surely die. For God knows that when you eat of it your eyes will be open, and you will be like God, knowing good and evil"* (Gen. 3:4–5). He slandered God and dismissed his threat as untruthful. We watch as Woman is dragged away and enticed by her own desire – which conceives and gives birth to sin (Jas. 1:14–15). She looked at the forbidden tree. She took, ate, served some to her husband, and he ate.

Most caregivers of children will tell you that no one has to teach a child to sin. Playrooms can testify that the smallest kid is capable of bitterness, wrath, anger, clamor, slander, along with every form of malice (Eph. 4:31). Sin is natural to us from infancy. Theologians call this "original sin" and it refers not to the initial transgression committed but to the *effects* of that first sin. God gave Adam and Woman rule over creation, so when they rebelled, their corruption impacted everything within the bounds of their dominion.[1] This includes us – people who originate from this earliest couple. We are sinners *not* merely because we sin but because we became *innately* sinful with that first bite of forbidden fruit.[2]

Woman swallowed that fruit and looked up to find deception. The meal had opened her eyes – not to wisdom but to the reality of her guilt and shame. She and Adam scurried about the garden, picking up fig leaves for covering (Gen. 3:7) Their sinful distrust of God had brought alienation between *them*. The shameless nudity of Genesis 2:25 was gone – and so was peace with *Yahweh Elohim*.

God judged Woman and Adam – but not without mercy. The snake, who dared to command unauthorized dominion in his garden, was cursed to crawl on his belly, always eating dust (Gen. 3:14). Woman, whom he sought to convert as an ally, was made his mortal enemy. She would bear a child who would crush his head. The serpent's attempt to strike back would land no higher than the Crusher's heel (Gen. 3:15).

Theologians call Genesis 3:15 the *protoevangelion* (the first gospel announcement). This is the earliest verse that declares a coming Savior. A Seed of the Woman would come to defeat the deceiving serpent. And from this point onward, Scripture begins to trace the woman's promised Seed in a line that passes through Seth, Noah, Abraham, Jacob's sons, and ultimately ends with Jesus Christ, the Son of God (Mt. 1:1–17; Lk. 3:23–38).

In many ways, the big story of Scripture surrounds this struggle between the offspring of the woman and the offspring of the serpent. Whether it's Cain against Abel (Gen. 4), Pharaoh against Israel (Ex. 1; 14), Goliath against David (1 Sam. 17), or the murderous religious leaders against Jesus (Jn. 8:39–44), the Bible shows the pattern of two communities of people: those redeemed by grace and those who oppose the redeemed. This cosmic battle is finally settled by the victorious work of Christ – that is, his life, death, resurrection, and second coming (Rev. 20:10). God was *gracious* to insert the depraved woman into this glorious drama of redemption!

Woman would die in time – but on *that* day, she's named Eve, mother of the *living* (Gen. 3:20). She and Adam would multiply as ordained at the beginning (Gen. 1:28). Eve would bring forth children in pain (Gen. 3:16). And she would do so outside of the garden. The first couple was driven out to work the ground east of Eden until death returned them back to dust (Gen. 3:23–24). But they didn't go empty handed. God replaced their wilting leaves with clothing of his own making (Gen. 3:20).

The woman who was serenaded at Creation was covered at the Fall. And the God of Genesis 3 continues to trade insufficient coverings for his own garment. Every woman who is tempted to hide her guilt and shame behind the false garbs of self-righteousness and self-help can rejoice. Eve's greatest son, the Seed of the Woman, exchanges our due condemnation for his own righteousness (2 Cor. 5:21). Today, God welcomes us – like our mother Eve – to receive the imperishable garment that he alone provides. His covering doesn't wilt and fade in this painful life east of Eden. Eve's story in Genesis 4 will testify to this.

3

Eve

Pain and hope in the wildernesses east of Eden

(Genesis 4)

Reflection

Pain enters the scene early in the story of redemption. It strikes Eve – but she could testify to this: we can have hope amid our pain because God keeps his word.

Eve had never known a moment outside of the garden. But there came a day when her eyes opened to a painful life east of Eden. What were her thoughts on that first morning, I wonder? Did she grieve loudly? Did remorse threaten to overwhelm her? Did she console herself with God's promise of a snake-crushing offspring? Her statement in Genesis 4:1 seems to suggest hope in God's faithfulness: *"Now Adam knew Eve his wife, and she conceived and bore Cain, saying, 'I have gotten a man with the help of the LORD.'"* God remembered her in the wilderness and by his mercy, the "mother of all living" became a mom (Gen. 3:20).

This woman – who had obeyed the voice of the cunning snake – deserved nothing but death. Yet there she was, alive and producing life.

Eve knew that her child was God-wrought and not the product of her own strength or merit. She called her son Cain. The name sounds like the Hebrew word for "gotten."[1] God had *given* her offspring – would this one be the serpent-crusher she longed for?

Tragically, what follows in Genesis 4 brings pain before consolation. Eve gave birth to a second son – Abel (Gen. 4:2). Her two boys grew up to be working men. Abel was a shepherd and Cain, a farmer. One day, both sons presented an offering to the Lord. Cain brought the fruit of the ground. Abel gave the firstborn of his flock (Gen. 4:3–4). God, who knows the intentions of every heart, *"had regard for Abel and his offering but for Cain and his offering he had no regard. So Cain was very angry, and his face fell"* (Gen. 4:4–5). And from here, the story turns and slips into sins that magnify the first parents' Fall.

Genesis 4 isn't a long chapter, and yet it contains an "abundance of recognizable human experiences."[2] We witness sibling rivalry, as envious Cain fumes over God's pleasure in his brother. We find distrust of God's Word as Cain ignores God's warnings against sinful anger. We see uncontrolled anger as it crouches, pounces, and masters Cain. There's domestic violence and murder as Cain strikes and kills his brother in a field (Gen. 4:6–8). The evil sown in Genesis 3:6 was reaping a bounty of depravity in the world – and pain in Eve's household.

I remember the first time I noticed a sin in my daughter that reminded me of my own past. My feelings were a jumble of present worries and former regrets. I can't help but mourn with Eve in Genesis 4. She is bereaved of both her sons: the second was dead and the first was his killer. *"In pain you shall bring forth children"* (Gen. 3:16). God's words perhaps rung in her ears at the news of Abel's death. Surely motherhood's pain is more than labor's contractions.[3] The child she had named "gotten with God's help" had taken the life of his brother. And the entire drama was a sad echo of her own earlier crime – only amplified in degree.

Like mother, like son – Cain supplanted divine sovereignty by stealing something God had created. Not fruit this time, but human life. Men and women were to fill the earth with people, not destroy them. And yet, we find Adam and Eve's firstborn son with bloody hands. The deadly effects of original sin produced an immediate escalation of sin.[4]

Cain was bold in his rebellion. God posed the same question asked of his mother in Genesis 3:13: "*What have you done*?" (Gen. 4:10). A cornered Eve had blamed another and then quietly received her judgment. Cain, on the other hand, denied any knowledge of the crime and then challenged the severity of his sentence (Gen. 4:13–14). In the end, a cursed Cain slithered further east to father descendants who would generate cities and cycles of corruption. We see the first polygamous marriage, violent revenge, and more murder in Cain's line (Gen. 4:16–24).

Eve was left behind with a dead son and a second who acted more snake-like than snake-crusher. Would God's grace continue to shine in this wilderness of pain? Where was the promised Seed of the Woman?

"*And Adam knew his wife again, and she bore a son and called his name Seth, for she said, 'God has appointed for me another offspring instead of Abel, for Cain killed him'*" (Gen. 4:25). Seth – whose name sounds like the Hebrew word for "appointed" – was placed in Eve's arms.[5] The Lord appointed another offspring – a seed who would grow to produce good fruit. The covenant line of Seth would lead to righteous Noah, Abraham, David, all the way down to a holy baby in a manger (Lk. 3:23–38). God would keep his promise. Eve didn't hope in vain.

Pain enters the scene early in the story of redemption. It strikes Eve – but she could testify to this: we can have hope amid our pain *because* God keeps his word. His poem of judgment to the serpent will be fully realized. The conquering Seed will crush the effects of sin and "*will wipe away every tear from [our] eyes, and death shall be no more, neither shall there be mourning, nor crying, nor pain anymore*" (Rev. 21:4). Pain has an end date. God's people, living in the wilderness east of Eden, can rest their hope in God's unfailing promises.

Just ask the daughters of Eve who follow her in the book of Genesis.

PART TWO:

Women of Genesis

4

Sarah

The weak matriarch and God's perfect strength

(Genesis 11:27 – 23:20)

Reflection

The woman introduced as barren gives birth to the son of promise and ultimately the Seed who trades our curses for his blessings. God's strength is made perfect in weakness.

The road between Genesis 5 and 12 is littered with death. We see the effects of the Fall as genealogies begin with birth announcements and end with obituaries (Gen. 5:1–31). People began to multiply on the face of the earth. Their corruption also multiplied (Gen. 6:5–7). God – who knows every word, deed, *and* thought – saw only evil continually and sent a flood to blot it out (Gen. 6:11–13). *"Everything on the dry land in whose nostrils was the breath of life died"* (Gen. 7:22). The consequences of the Fall are staggering – but so is God's grace.

The Lord preserved one man and his family: Noah. A descendant of Seth, Noah is introduced to us in Scripture with a sense of expectation.

His father, Lamech, says of him in Genesis 5:29: *"Out of the ground that the LORD has cursed, this one shall bring us relief from our work and from the painful toil of our hands."* Could Noah be the promised Seed of Genesis 3:15? Would *he* crush the deceiver and overturn the effects of the curse?

Lamech's hope seemed promising until Genesis 9:20–27. There, we find Noah drunk, naked, shamed by his son Ham, and pouring down a curse on Canaan – Ham's son. In other words, the curse doesn't diminish but rather extends at the end of Noah's story. He died like his fathers before him (Gen. 9:29) – and the genealogies continued (Gen. 10; 11:10–32). It's at this point that we meet Sarai.

In a section full of lineages, we meet a woman introduced to us as barren and childless (Gen. 11:30). Sarai was the wife of Abram, a descendant of Terah, Noah, Seth, and Adam – the covenant line. Like many women, she would have entered marriage in anticipation of children. Sadly, for Sarai, the years passed without pregnancy. Family and neighbors perhaps ended their questions on children as they came to realize the truth: Sarai was a barren woman. The consequences of the curse bring death – not just to men but – to wombs.

Scripture chronicles the journey of Abram and Sarai with numerous stories. We have 13 chapters between their introduction in Genesis 11 and Sarai's death in Genesis 23 – a span of sixty-two years.[1] As we will see, the stories told within these years paint the picture of a new kind of "Adam and Eve" who also prove weak – and the God who declares weak sinners righteous by faith.

It begins in Genesis 12:1–3 with the call of Abram. Of all the men in pagan Haran, *Yahweh Elohim* visited Abram with a command and a promise:

> *Go from your country and your kindred and your father's house to the land that I will show you. And I will make you a great nation, and I will bless you and make your name great, so that you will be a blessing. I will*

bless those who bless you, and him who dishonors you I will curse, and in you all the families of the earth shall be blessed.

This marks an incredible place in redemptive history. God promised to make Abram a "great nation" – a covenant people for his own possession. He would extend his blessings to all the families of the earth through the Seed produced from this nation. Unbeknown to Abram, God's work to cancel the effects of the curse had begun – and he was using this childless man in his great plan of redemption.

What thoughts crept into Sarai's mind as she pondered this news? Did she wonder how a man without a descendant would become an entire nation? Did God's amazing promise grow fresh expectation in her heart? Would she at last know the joy of motherhood? Or would God increase Abram without Sarai? Was there fear instead of hope?

The couple journeyed through Canaan and, after ten years, God met with Abram again. He reaffirmed his promise of an offspring and sealed his word with a covenant (Gen. 15:1–21). Here, we witness Sarai's inability to reconcile God's promise to Abram with her own barrenness.

Sarai speaks in Genesis 16:2 (the first time we hear a woman since Eve): *"Behold now, the LORD has prevented me from bearing children. Go in to my servant; it may be that I shall obtain children by her."* Like Eve, who took and gave something forbidden to her husband, Sarai took and gave her maidservant Hagar to Abram as her surrogate.[2] And like Adam, Abram listened to the voice of his wife (Gen. 3:17; 16:2). This polygamous move – first seen among Cain's wicked offspring (Gen. 4:19) – proved disastrous (Gen. 16:1–16). Ishmael (Abram's firstborn by Hagar) was born and with him, contention in the household. Hagar began to disrespect Sarai and Sarai responded with harshness. In the end, the scheme ushered the pain and alienation promised in Genesis 3:16.

Thirteen years after Ishmael's birth, God changed ninety-nine-year-old Abram's name to Abraham and eighty-nine-year-old Sarai's name to Sarah.[3] And for the first time since their now twenty-four-year journey began, Sarah was *directly* mentioned in God's promise to Abraham: *"I will give you a son by her, and she shall become nations; kings of people shall come from her"* (Gen. 17:15–21). Sarah's womb would produce life. The idea to her was laughable, she was worn out and her husband was old (Gen. 18:12–14). But nothing is too hard for the Lord.

Within a year, Sarah conceived Isaac. His name means "laughter." God turned the source of Sarah's laughter from cynicism to joy (Gen. 21:6–7). And her laughter reminds us that God's gift of children is never given because of our works, but by his grace. Human reproduction, like spiritual regeneration, is ultimately the merciful work of the living God (Jn. 1:12–13). And every child born to the descendants of rebellious Adam and Eve is evidence of God's unmerited mercy.

A weak, yet believing, woman is useful to God. Sarah's image hangs in Hebrews' Hall of Faith as one who considered God faithful to his promise (Heb. 11:11). Her faith in Scripture appears small at times, but we are saved by the *object* of our faith and not by the size of it. In Sarah, we see that God's strength is made perfect in weakness (2 Cor. 12:9). The woman introduced to us as barren gives birth to the son of promise. From her womb comes a great nation and eventually the Seed who would do what Noah couldn't – crush the serpent and trade our curses for his blessings. God made weak Sarah a matriarch of faith. He is kind. And as we will see in our next chapter, even Hagar can tell you that.

5

Hagar

The opening of Hagar's eyes

(Genesis 16 and 21:1–21)

Reflection

Those who look upon the God of Israel in trust are given sight to see the Living One who sees them. But those who trust in idols become as unseeing as their gods.

In Genesis 16:1, the author does something strange. He notes Sarah's barrenness again – but then introduces us to Hagar, as though she's part of the solution. This strange introduction of an Egyptian slave at odds with her mistress might cause us to wonder who exactly this servant was. Had she ever known freedom or was she born into servitude? Had she, in her captivity, found a sense of belonging in Abraham's camp? What exactly was her role in the household, and did she get along with Sarah? Scripture doesn't answer these questions. But here's one we might find an answer for: how long had Hagar been in Sarah's service before being made a concubine to Abraham, her husband?

We read of famine in Genesis 12:10–16. Abraham traveled from Canaan to Egypt to avoid it. Fearing that the Egyptians might kill him for his beautiful wife, he presented Sarah as his sister. Pharaoh was indeed captured by her beauty and took Sarah for his harem. He dealt well with Abraham for Sarah's sake and gave him large gifts of servants and livestock. The Lord, in his holiness, inflicted Pharaoh's household with plagues until Sarah's marital status was revealed and the woman was rejoined to her husband. Most commentators place Hagar among the Egyptian servants given during this period in Egypt. If so, Hagar met Sarah in Genesis 12:16 and journeyed with her until named to us in Genesis 16:1 – a span of around ten years.

Ten years is a long time to serve someone. How did Sarah treat Hagar in those years? Was her harshness in Genesis 16:6 a totally new dynamic? Did Sarah's general manner reflect a fear of the God who would inspire Ephesians 6:9? *"Masters ... stop your threatening, knowing that he who is both their Master and yours is in heaven, and that there is no partiality with him."* Again, we don't know. It's reasonable to consider this however: a mistress who wanted to obtain a child through a servant was likely to select one she trusted (consider Abraham's great confidence in his head servant in Genesis 24:1–9).

If this was the case with Sarah and Hagar, then we must mourn the devastating effects of sin as we witness Hagar's scorn and Sarah's abuse in Genesis 16:4–6. God's Word is wise: *"Therefore a man shall leave his father and his mother and hold fast to his wife, and they shall become one flesh"* (Gen. 2:24). As the story continues, God proves not only his wisdom, but also his grace.

Hagar conceived a child with Abraham – and the strife between her and Sarah sent her running. She was found by the angel of the Lord at the well leading to Shur – a fort on the border of Egypt.[1] The angel of the Lord told Hagar to return to Sarah and submit to her. Hagar obeyed, showing that her submission was ultimately to One higher than Sarah (Eph. 6:5). The angel's command came with gracious words:

Yahweh Elohim had heard Hagar's affliction. She would bear a son named Ishmael (meaning "God hears"). God would multiply Hagar's offspring without number (Gen. 16:7–12).

Hagar saw, listened, and then opened her mouth: *"So she called the name of the* Lord *who spoke to her, 'You are a God of seeing,' for she said, 'Truly here I have seen him who looks after me'"* (Gen. 16:13). Hagar named the well Beer-lahai-roi – the well of the Living One who sees me. Eve's first recorded words in Scripture altered God's command by adding a prohibition never given (Gen. 3:2–3). Sarah, the second woman we hear in the Bible, spoke to incite polygamy (Gen. 15:2). Hagar is the third woman to speak in Scripture and her words testify of God's gracious eye and care. This captive foreigner is the first woman to praise God in the Bible.

Other questions spring up at this point. What was Hagar's view of Abraham's God prior to this divine encounter? Had she always seen him as the *living* God who sees? Or did she wonder about this invisible deity – so elusive next to the engraved idols of Egypt? If the latter, how amazing to witness the opening of Hagar's eyes. Psalm 115:2–9 says this:

> *Why should the nations say, "Where is their God?" Our God is in the heavens; he does all that he pleases. Their idols are silver and gold, the work of human hands. They have mouths, but do not speak; eyes, but do not see. They have ears, but do not hear; noses, but do not smell. They have hands, but do not feel; feet, but do not walk; and they do not make a sound in their throat. Those who make them become like them; so do all who trust in them. O Israel, trust in the* Lord*! He is their help and their shield.*

Those who look upon the God of Israel in trust are given sight to see the Living One who sees them. But those who trust in idols become as unseeing as their gods. In Hagar, we see the Living One who graciously opens the eyes of blind sinners – including those of an Egyptian woman.

Hagar left Abraham's household again in Genesis 21:1–14 – only this time, she was sent away. Abraham rose early in the morning to see her off. Hagar was instantly a single mother with a son to raise. What was her sorrow as she walked away that day? The burden of solo parenting was immediate as she and her son stumbled around in the wilderness of Beersheba, dehydrated and near death. Hagar and her boy lifted their voices and cried – and the God of Beer-lahai-roi heard them. He came down and opened her eyes to see a well of water (Gen. 21:15–19). She and her son would live.

God's promised redeemer doesn't come through Hagar – that gracious honor goes to Sarah. Isaac's line would carry the promised Seed of the Woman, not Ishmael's (Gen. 21:12). But God, for Abraham's sake, doesn't abandon this mother and her son (Gen. 21:13, 20). His desire to bless all the families of the earth through Abraham is seen in his merciful compassion toward Hagar (Gen. 12:3). Her account may prompt questions but there is no questioning God's willing care for this Egyptian woman. He is indeed the sustainer of all who look to him. If so, let your eyes rest solely on the living God who sees you. For he is our help and our shield!

6

Rebekah

The "happily-ever-after" we long for

(Genesis 24 – 27 and 28:1–9)

Reflection

The deception that began in Eden crept its way into Rebekah's family. But the God of Eden was also there – and his Genesis 3:15 promise is not overcome by the sin of Adam's offspring.

Sarah gave birth for the first time at ninety years old and died at the age of 127 (Gen. 23:1). This means she had thirty-seven years to dote on her boy – the son of promise. Isaac must have missed his mother terribly at her death. A chapter after Sarah's burial, we find Abraham instructing his chief servant to go seek a wife for Isaac (Gen. 24:4). A bride might comfort Isaac. But even more, a wife meant the promise of offspring would continue (Gen. 3:15; 12:1–3).

The servant was to travel to Abraham's native country and family in search of Isaac's bride (Gen. 24:1–9). The woman would be a descendant of Noah, Seth, and Adam – the covenant line of promise. The chief servant traveled for hundreds of miles to the city where Abraham's brother Nahor lived (Gen. 24:15). The servant arrived just as the women of the town were fetching water from the spring. God is sovereign – right down to his timing.

The servant, likely Eliezer of Damascus (Gen. 15:2), was careful with his mission. He prayed asking God to reveal his choice of a wife from among the women: *"Let the young woman to whom I shall say, 'Please let down your jar that I may drink,' and who shall say, 'Drink, and I will water your camels' – let her be the one whom you have appointed for your servant Isaac"* (Gen. 24:14). Before the prayer was done, Rebekah, the beautiful granddaughter of Nahor, came walking by. The man sought a drink, and, without hesitation, Rebekah offered water to him – *and* his camels (Gen. 24:15–21). Now, a single camel can hold up to twenty-five gallons of water. Rebekah worked to quench *ten* of these animals – showing a hospitality that might rival the most genial ancient Near Eastern welcome.

Rebekah was betrothed to Isaac with the consent of her father Bethuel and her brother Laban (Gen. 24:50–51). Like her great uncle Abraham before her, she willingly left home, country, and family for an unknown land (Gen. 12:1). She was escorted to her husband who received her with love. Isaac took Rebekah into the tent of Sarah and was consoled by his wife after the death of his mother (Gen. 24:67). Sadly, this sweet beginning would grow bitter over time.

Rebekah resembled Sarah in one key way – infertility. Isaac married at the age of forty but didn't father children until the age of sixty (Gen. 25:20; 26). Barrenness – Sarah's frustration – plagued Rebekah for twenty long years. In the end, Isaac prayed for his wife and God opened her womb with twins. Carrying multiples is never easy but Rebekah must have had a particularly difficult pregnancy. Scripture says this: *"The children struggled together within her, and she said, '...why is this happening to me?' So she went to inquire of the LORD"* (Gen. 25:22). And God gave a surprising answer.

The Lord told Rebekah that she was carrying twins – brothers who would be divided. God's elective purposes would prevail over custom, and the firstborn would serve the second. The Abrahamic blessing of land and seed would be granted to Jacob, the younger, over Esau, the older (Gen. 25:23).

Did Rebekah share this news with her husband? If so, Isaac appeared to ignore the message. He favored his son Esau and resolved to bless him rather than Jacob. When Rebekah learned of this decision, she plotted to overrule her husband. She disguised Jacob as Esau, and the younger son was blessed in place of the elder (Gen. 27:1–29). The effects of the curse on marriage hover in this chapter as contrary desires conspire for control (Gen. 3:16).

Rebekah believed God's Word but didn't look to the Lord himself to prove it. The choice of Jacob was ultimately God's – not hers. He elects people for his own purposes and according to the counsel of his own will (Eph. 1:11). Perhaps God would have displayed his providence in some glorious way had Rebekah called Jacob for prayer rather than for scheming. Certainly, Scripture (see the book of Esther) gives evidence of God's prevailing word over a person's determination. Instead, Rebekah sought to bring God's oracle to pass by her own wisdom. The result was a feud on the scale of Cain's and Abel's. Scornful Esau decided to kill his brother and Jacob was forced to flee the family at his threat (Gen. 27:41–46). Like Eve, Rebekah lost a son to the vengeance of his brother (Gen. 4:8).

Isaac and Rebekah's narrative is the stuff of movies. A beautiful maiden was providentially chosen by God through her incredible hospitality. She courageously left her home for a new land. She entered marriage with the promise of love – and even the bitterness of infertility was chased away by the gift of twins. There should have been a "happily-ever-after" ending to this story. Rather, the author tells the account not as a fairy tale, but as the drama of a post-Genesis 3 family. There's discord in marriage, favoritism among parents, sibling rivalry, crafty lies, and threats of death. The deception that began in Eden crept its way to Genesis 24 – 28 and into Rebekah's family.

But the God of Eden is also in these chapters. And his Genesis 3:15 promise is not overcome by the sin of Adam's offspring. The Abrahamic blessing of land and seed was passed on to Jacob. God's promise lived on. The snake-crusher – a distant son of Rebekah herself – would come. And his perfect work on behalf of sinners will bring the happily-ever-after for which our souls long (Rev. 21:4–5). Women living in post-Genesis 3 families and communities can call on him with a sure hope.

7

Rachel

The struggles of a desperate housewife

(Genesis 29 – 35)

Reflection

God's promised Seed comes to deal with our deadly enemies – including the insidious idols we crave.

What do *Sheol* (the grave), a barren womb, fire, and the land have in common? My question isn't a setup for a terrible joke, but a reference to Proverbs 30:15b-16:

> *Three things are never satisfied;*
> *four never say, "Enough":*
> *Sheol, the barren womb,*
> *the land never satisfied with water,*
> *and the fire that never says, "Enough."*

This passage is incredibly vivid. It compares the hunger of an infertile womb to the insatiable nature of death, fire's desire for more, and the land's unquenchable thirst. Here again we behold poetry's ability to paint a graphic picture with few words. But if a narrative can also capture the longing of a womb, then Rachel's is that story.

Like her aunt Rebekah before her, Rachel's account began like a fairy tale. Her cousin Jacob escaped the vengeance of his brother Esau to find shelter with her father Laban in Paddan-aram (Gen. 28:5). Rachel was the first relative Jacob met at the end of his journey. She walked to a well with her father's sheep and encountered an eager Jacob. He pushed the stone away from the entrance of the well and watered her animals – as his mother had done many years before him for Abraham's servant (Gen. 24:18–20; 29:1–12). Jacob remained with the family and agreed to serve Laban seven years in exchange for Rachel's hand in marriage. Genesis 29:15–20 tells us that the seven years faded as mere days for Jacob because of his great love for Rachel. Sadly, these tender verses are followed by terrible strife.

Laban gave Leah – Rachel's older sister – to Jacob instead of his intended. Laban's stated reason for this deception is interesting when you remember Jacob's trick to seize his elder brother's birthright: *"It is not done in our country, to give the younger before the firstborn. Complete the week of this one, and we will give you the other also in return for serving me another seven years"* (Gen. 29:26–27). Laban throws Rachel into the family portrait at the end of Leah's bridal week and Jacob became the husband of two wives within days. This new family structure was the setting for the battle of the sisters.

The sibling rivalries we saw earlier – Cain and Abel, and Jacob and Esau – took an awful twist as these women struggled for the favor and seed of Jacob. Rachel held his affections, but Leah had the advantage of fertility. Rachel was found to be barren while her sister wobbled around, her belly bouncing with life, birthing one baby after another.

We read in Genesis 30:1: *"When Rachel saw that she bore Jacob no children, she envied her sister. She said to Jacob, 'Give me children, or I shall die!'"* These words are packed with emotion. Thoughts of pregnancy must have consumed Rachel. Each month brought a fresh hope and then the bloody reality of her emptiness. I can't help but remember God's poem to Woman: *"In pain you shall bring forth children."* The pain of Genesis 3:16 includes infertility as much as it does labor contractions. The effects of the Fall are here – but so is God's mercy.

The Lord worked behind the scenes of this drama to deliver his promise of offspring for Abraham (Gen. 12:2; 15:5). In many ways, Genesis 29:31 – 30:24 is a genealogical record in narrative form. God was building the great nation through which his conquering Savior would come. His purposes in salvation triumph despite the effects of the curse – seen in this family's polygamy, favoritism, competition, envy, and bitter barrenness. In fact, God's loving-kindness and sovereignty shines brighter as the story darkens.

Rachel thickened the plot by giving her maidservant to Jacob as a concubine. She says in Genesis 30:3: *"Here is my servant Bilhah; go in to her, so that she may give birth on my behalf, that even I may have children through her."* Like her grandmother-in-law Sarah before her – and like her sister Leah after her (Gen. 30:9–13) – Rachel placed her servant in her husband's arms as her surrogate. Bilhah had two sons (Dan and Naphtali) on behalf of Rachel (Gen. 30:5–8). But the insatiable womb craved on as she turned to an interesting fertility treatment – mandrakes.

Mandrakes were orange-colored fruit that were superstitiously thought to be fertility-inducing.[1] Leah's eldest son, Reuben, found the fruit during harvest and brought them to his mother. Rachel was so eager for the effects of the fruit that she traded her night with Jacob for the mandrakes. She said: *"he may lie with you tonight in exchange for your son's mandrakes"* (Gen. 30:15). And sadly for Rachel, it was her sister who conceived that evening (Gen. 30:14–18). God's purposes prevail over desperate moves – for *"Unless the Lord builds the house, those who build it labor in vain ... children are a heritage from [him]"* (Ps. 127:1, 3). Rachel turned from the mandrakes to prayer and God heard her.

Following the birth of ten sons and at least one daughter (Dinah) to Jacob by three other women, God remembered Rachel and listened to her. He opened her womb, and she conceived and bore a son (Gen. 30:22–23). She welcomed her firstborn, Joseph, and credited God for removing her reproach. Yes, the shame was gone... but not the yearning. Joseph, which means "may God add another" is not only a name but also a prayer – a plea to God for more children (Gen. 30:24).

And perhaps it was this craving for more that lured Rachel to her father's gods. After twenty years of service, Jacob left Laban for Canaan (Gen. 31:1–21).[2] Rachel stole her father's household gods before departing (Gen. 31:19). Some commentators believe that these were figurines of nude goddesses that signaled special protection or guaranteed fertility for the bearer.[3] If so, perhaps Rachel's hope for children compelled her to seek some "extra security" in addition to the Lord? We can't say for certain. Yet, how closely she resembled her future progeny as she slipped those idols into her belongings.

Israel would waver between true and false worship throughout her history. We see moments of syncretism in the Old Testament, when God's people merge their worship of *Yahweh* with that of Canaanite deities (Ex. 32:1–5; 1 Kgs. 18:21). Perhaps this was Rachel's struggle in Genesis 31. She praised God for her children and yet kept her father's idols. Jacob told Laban that whoever took his gods would be put to death (Gen. 31:25–35). Rachel was never found with them – and yet she soon died. Rachel experienced a difficult labor with her second son, Benjamin, and passed away giving birth to the very baby she so desperately wanted (Gen. 35:16–21). She was buried on the road to Ephrath (that is, Bethlehem).

Centuries after her death, the prophet Jeremiah remembered Rachel as he assured the Israelites of God's plan to turn mourning to joy. Israel, like a longing mother, grieved for its exiled children and refused to be comforted (Jer. 31:15). But God would bring restoration to his people (Jer. 31:16–17). Matthew recalls this in his Gospel when he quotes

Jeremiah 31. The mothers of Bethlehem wept over the slaughtered bodies of their young sons, killed by brutal Herod. But God's promised salvation was at hand. Restoration and eternal salvation were coming through the Son sent to deal with Israel's deadly enemies – including her idolatrous sins.

Dear friend, whenever we wrap our ultimate value, joy, identity, or need around anything – except the Lord – we have molded an idol. We can even worship God's good gifts – children, marriage, a job, food – as if we were worshiping God himself. But God's promised Savior came east of Eden to uproot the idolatrous sins of those who trust in him. May our hearts long for this Savior like a barren womb that hungers for life.

8

Leah

Leah's eyes were weak but her God was strong

(Genesis 29 – 35 and 49:31)

Reflection

Afflicted Leah became the ancestral mother of the Man of Sorrows – a Savior who can sympathize with the rejected.

I can't help but sympathize with Leah. Imagine being compared with your sister in this way: *"Leah's eyes were weak, but Rachel was beautiful in form and appearance"* (Gen. 29:17).

Here's a woman known for weak eyes while her younger sister is recognized for her beauty. Now whether your commentary interprets Leah's "weak eyes" as a positive feature (tender and delicate) or a negative flaw (pale or poor sighted), the contrast between the two is clear: Rachel was good-looking, and Leah wasn't the belle of the ball.[1]

How soon did Leah notice the differences between her and Rachel? Did she hear whispered remarks growing up? "There goes Rachel, the pretty one – and Leah, the one with the weak eyes." If Leah was jealous of Rachel in their youth, those feelings heightened with the appearance of their cousin Jacob in Genesis 29. A month after he arrived, Jacob declared his desire for Rachel and offered to serve her father, Laban, seven years for her hand (Gen. 29:14–18). Laban agreed and Jacob got to work (Gen. 29:19–20). The prize of Rachel was enough to energize him on and the seven years passed like days.

But to Jacob's disappointment, *Leah* – not Rachel – was given to him at the end of the set time. Laban tossed Rachel into the mix (for another seven years of service) when questioned. His greed for Jacob's labor entrapped the latter in a polygamous marriage against his will, with two sisters from the same house. One he adored and the other, he hated (Gen. 29:21–35). Note that the Mosaic law will later forbid the marrying of two living sisters (Lev. 18:18). But for now, poor Leah awoke to a marriage with a man who didn't want her – and likely resented her for being the object of her father's deceit.

Leah was a third wheel in her own household. Her husband slept with her but didn't honor her with love. What tears those weak eyes must have shed! Jacob didn't regard her – but *God* saw her. *"When the Lord saw that Leah was hated, he opened her womb, but Rachel was barren"* (Gen. 29:31). The giver of life enabled her to bear six sons and at least one daughter, Dinah (Gen. 30:19–21). The names of her sons are telling. They testify to her hope and her great suffering.

Leah conceived four sons in rapid succession in Genesis 29:32–34 – the names of the initial three are heartbreaking. She called her firstborn Reuben (a combination of the Hebrew words "look" and "a son") saying: *"Because the Lord has looked upon my affliction; for now my husband will love me."* She named her second Simeon ("to hear") saying: *"Because the Lord has heard that I am hated, he has given me this son also."* The third she called Levi ("to join") saying: *"Now this time my husband will be attached to me, because I have borne him three sons."* Leah's hope for love at Levi's birth failed. Jacob didn't trade her affection for sons. She resigned then, with her fourth, to simply praise the Lord and he's named Judah ("praised").[2]

No doubt, Leah's worship that day carried a thread of grief. And Jacob's attentions will further divide as we continue.

Rachel gave her maidservant Bilhah to Jacob as a concubine, and she bore two sons. Leah, desiring more children, handed over *her* own servant, Zilpah, and two additional sons (Gad and Asher) were born (Gen. 30:9–13). God listened once more to Leah's prayers and opened her womb to two more sons. Issachar was conceived the night she swapped mandrakes with Rachel for Jacob's bed and Zebulun became her last son and final (vain) hope for Jacob's love (Gen. 30:16–20). Leah's story is filled with pregnancies, rivalries, and disappointments. In her, we see again that Genesis 3:16 is indeed more than labor contractions and infertility. She shows us that a mom with an uncaring husband knows what it means to bring forth children in pain.

And indeed, Leah was a woman who knew sorrow. Just consider this: she was treated as an object of deceit by her own father; her husband didn't love her; she suffered the rape of her daughter Dinah in Genesis 34:1–2 and then the murderous revenge of her sons against an entire city (Gen. 34:3–31); she must have felt the shame of Reuben's illicit sexual encounter with Bilhah (Gen. 35:22); and witnessed the agonizing death of her sister in childbirth (Gen. 35:16–19). Leah knew agony.

But God was nearby.

God remembered this rejected woman in fulfilling his purposes for salvation. The nation of Israel comprises twelve tribes – half of whom came through Leah. In her death, she was honored with a place among the patriarchs and matriarchs of Israel. Rachel died between Bethel and Ephrath and was buried "along the way" but Leah was put to rest in the Promised Land – next to her husband Jacob in the burial place of Abraham's lineage (Gen. 35:16–19; 49:29–32).

Much more, Leah gave birth to Judah, the one through whom the promised Seed of the Woman would come (Mt. 1:2–3). She became the ancestral mother of the Man of Sorrows. This man – like Leah, although to a greater degree – was despised by those who should have loved him. Hear Isaiah 53:2b-3: *"He had no form or majesty that we should look at him, and no beauty that we should desire him. He was despised and rejected by men; a man of sorrows, and acquainted with grief; and as one from whom men hide their faces he was despised, and we esteemed him not."* Leah's greater Son walked the path of pain and rejection and can bear our griefs (Is. 53:4).

Yes, Leah's eyes were weak, but they were fixed on a strong God. She spoke to the Lord in her suffering, and he listened to her (Gen. 30:17). The Man of Sorrows can sympathize with our weaknesses. He was made like us in every respect, *"so that he might become a merciful and faithful high priest in the service of God"* (Heb. 2:17). So *"Let us then with confidence draw near to the throne of grace, that we may receive mercy and find grace to help in time of need"* (Heb. 4:16). God is the hope of the forsaken. Let the afflicted be encouraged today.

9

Tamar

God's blessings flow wherever the curse is found

(Genesis 38)

Reflection

The matriarchs and patriarchs of Genesis were sinners who endured in faith, trusting God's promises – promises that are ultimately fulfilled by his Son, our substitute.

Judah was Jacob's fourth son by Leah. He must have been a persuasive man – his voice convinced his brothers to sell Joseph into Egyptian slavery (Gen. 37:1–28). They deceived their father, Jacob, into believing Joseph was dead. After this set of events, Judah – perhaps to avoid an inconsolable Jacob (Gen. 37:35) – left his brothers and settled near a Canaanite friend named Hirah (Gen. 38:1).

Judah met and married a Canaanite woman and their union produced three sons: Er, Onan, and Shelah. Er grew up and Judah found a Canaanite wife for him: Tamar. *"But Er, Judah's firstborn, was wicked in the sight of the LORD, and the LORD put him to death"* (Gen. 38:7). The precise nature of Er's wickedness isn't given. Yet Scripture reminds us here of God's condemnation of sin. His kindness is always meant to lead sinners to repentance, not to embolden evil (Rom. 2:4). Tamar became a widow by God's justice.

What was it like being married to wicked Er? How did he treat Tamar? Did she fear him? Did she love him? Did she grieve from the heart at his passing – or was she relieved? We can't say. But this much we know: as Judah's firstborn, Er had the birthright to his inheritance. So, whatever her situation, Tamar at least had some security as the wife of Judah's future heir.

And the inheritance may have been substantial for we're later told of Judah's signet and cord (Gen. 38:18). These items belonged to men of significance. A signet was a cylinder seal worn on a cord around the neck. It served as the signature of a prominent man. He would seal contracts by rolling the cylinder over clay.[1] Judah's inheritance (whatever its exact worth) was large enough for Onan, his second son, to want it for himself. And Onan would exploit Tamar in his greed.

As the brother of a childless deceased man, Onan was expected to marry Tamar. The practice was called a levirate marriage (Deut. 25:5–10). The firstborn son of this union was considered the heir of the deceased. In the case of our story, Er's name would continue in Israel through a son born to Onan and Tamar. The child would also receive Er's birthright and with it, Judah's inheritance. The arrangement would keep the widow within the family (as we will see in the story of Ruth). This levirate custom obliged Onan to care for Tamar. But in a selfish move to maintain his new position as eldest and heir, he used her for sex but spilt his semen in the act. He discarded the seed God had promised as offspring to Abraham – and Eve before him (Gen. 15:5; 3:15). Onan acted wickedly *"in the sight of the Lord, and he put him to death also"* (Gen. 38:10).

God is holy.

Judah lost two corrupt sons but still failed to perceive God's holiness. Instead, he turned to Tamar in suspicion: two dead husbands had to mean a cursed wife – after all, Noah *had* cursed Canaan (Gen. 9:25). Fearing for the life of his last remaining son, he told Tamar to go and stay in her father's household as a widow (Gen. 38:11). Judah promised Shelah as a husband, once grown, but didn't keep his word (Gen. 38:12–14).

A daughter was supposed to leave her father's house and establish life in another family. She wasn't expected to return childless, impoverished, bereaved of two husbands, and presumably full of bad luck. Oh, how the town must have gossiped about poor Tamar. She was likely the topic of the rumor mill for weeks: the once wife of Judah's prominent heir, now a widow in her father's home with no prospect of a husband or child. Girl, you don't say!

The outcast Tamar was languishing away from God's covenant family because of superstition and neglect of duty. God had promised to bless Abraham and his offspring (Gen. 12:1–3). This blessing would extend to all the families of the earth – wherever the curse is found. We caught a glimpse of this when God sustained Hagar and her boy for Abraham's sake (Gen. 21:13, 20). Would this blessing stretch to Tamar too? For now, she seemed forgotten and forsaken by Judah. So, Tamar – after the manner of Rebekah (Gen. 27:6–10) – decided to take matters into her own hands. She used deception to right the wrong. And like Rebekah, God worked behind her scheme to fulfil his covenant purposes.

Apparently knowing her father-in-law's sexual vices (as well as her own ovulation cycle) Tamar disguised herself as a prostitute with the hope of receiving a child by Judah. "*When Judah saw her, he thought she was a prostitute, for she had covered her face. He turned to her at the roadside and said, 'Come, let me come in to you,'*" (Gen. 38:15–16). Tamar requested his signet, cord, and staff as a pledge for later payment and Judah handed them over. She took the items, but her wish is for pregnancy, not payment, and she got it. Judah impregnated his daughter-in-law without knowing it (Gen. 38:18).

Tamar's pregnancy was discovered at the start of her second trimester. A report went out to Judah: "*Tamar your daughter-in-law has been immoral. Moreover, she is pregnant by immorality"* (Gen. 38:24). An angry Judah sentenced her to death by fire. Tamar sent Judah's signet, cord, and staff to him as she was being dragged out of her father's house: *"By the man to whom these belong, I am pregnant"* (Gen. 38:25). Judah was forced to admit his role and failure of responsibility: *"She is more righteous than I, since I did not give her to my son Shelah"* (Gen. 38:26).

Tamar lived to deliver twin boys (Perez and Zerah). Judah didn't marry nor sleep with Tamar again, but she was grafted into the covenant family and mentioned in Israel's history (Ruth 4:12). Her son Perez would continue the genealogy that would lead to the Savior, making Tamar a distant mother of the promised Seed (Mt. 1:3). We can rejoice for this but there's still a question that begs an answer.

In this short chapter where two people, Er and Onan, are killed for wicked acts, why do deceitful Tamar and promiscuous Judah live? After all, God is a just judge. He doesn't sweep anything under a rug, punishing one transgression while ignoring another (Deut. 10:17). Every sin ever committed will be accounted for and rightly judged. God's righteous wrath will either fall on the sinner or it will be placed on God's perfect substitute (1 Jn. 2:2). So why does God kill Er and Onan but spare Tamar and Judah? The text doesn't give a direct answer – but we know this: the matriarchs and patriarchs of Genesis were sinners who endured in faith, trusting God's promises (Heb. 11:8–12) – promises ultimately fulfilled by his Son, our substitute. Some see Tamar's determination to preserve Judah's seed as evidence of faithfulness.[2] This may be so, but we can't say for certain. In the case of Judah, however, there is some biblical evidence of transformation as the story continues.

The man who sold his brother into slavery stood before that brother again in Genesis 44:14–34. He lifted his voice – not to incite sin this time but – to offer himself as a substitute for another in judgment. Judah points us here to his greater Son, born of Tamar. He, Jesus, is the hope of every sinner born east of Eden. Our many sins are forgiven in him and the righteousness we desperately long for comes through him alone. So, sinful saints, persevere in faith, trusting in Christ. He comes to make his blessings flow, wherever the curse is found.

The women of the Exodus will agree in Part Three of this book.

PART THREE:

Women of the Exodus

10

Shiphrah and Puah

The midwives and the snake-king

(Exodus 1)

Reflection

God's purposes cannot be thwarted. They often shine brightest in the shadow of threats and trials.

When we step from Genesis to Exodus, we find that the people – Adam and Eve's descendants; Abraham and Sarah's lineage; Isaac and Rebekah's offspring; Jacob, Rachel, and Leah's children; and the descendants of Judah and Tamar – have multiplied from a group of about seventy men into a vast nation (Ex. 1:1–7). They had traveled from Canaan to Egypt to escape famine in the days of Joseph, Egypt's second-in-command (Gen. 41; 46). Now, nearly four hundred years later, they have multiplied to fill the land (Gen. 15:13; Ex. 1:7). Israel was brimming with people – but her matriarchs and patriarchs were gone.

Exodus 1:6 says: "*Then Joseph died, and all his brothers and all that generation.*" Every human character we meet in Genesis is dead by Exodus.

Like a film sequel with a new cast, the show continues without the actors we've known. How different would this next season be? Exodus 1 answers this question with an important reminder: people may pass, but God's promises do not.

God's covenant with Abraham was *"an everlasting covenant for his offspring after him"* (Gen. 17:7, 19). Dead fathers didn't mean a dead Israel. The great nation that would produce an offspring to bless all the families of the earth was budding (Gen. 12:1–3). The term "Israelite" (or "the people of Israel") is rarely used in the book of Genesis – but that is not the case in Exodus. The title is repeatedly mentioned, four times in Chapter 1 alone (Ex. 1:7, 9, 12, 13). A strong nation was emerging, but a snake rose to swallow her at birth.

The pharaoh of Exodus 1 appears as a serpentine figure in this narrative (Gen. 3:15). Cultural context tells us that the man wore a crown with an *uraeus* (a reared cobra) attached.[1] This new king – either ignorant or dismissive of Joseph's role in Egyptian history – saw Israel's population boom as a national security threat. These mighty people were distinct from his own. What would keep them from joining Egypt's enemies in a time of war? The question conjured fears and schemes in Pharaoh's heart, and he brutally enslaved Israel to reduce her numbers (Ex. 1:10–14). But his plan exposed a glorious paradox: God's purposes often shine brightest in the shadow of trials.

As seen throughout church history, God's people can multiply and spread amid oppression because of God's faithfulness. Persecuted Christians in the Roman Empire and the church in communist China could testify to this – and so does Israel in Exodus 1. God's covenant purposes prevailed over the terror of the Egyptian state. Thus *"the more they were oppressed, the more [Israel] multiplied and the more they spread abroad"* (Ex. 1:12). Pharaoh's Plan A fell flat – and he moved on to Plan B. His second plot would involve two ordinary Hebrew women, midwives named Shiphrah and Puah.

We meet Shiphrah and Puah in Exodus 1:15–22. Midwives are natural in a baby boom story. But these ladies were initially called to kill – not to aid life. Pharoah's command to them was this: *"When you serve as midwife to the Hebrew women and see them on the birthstool, if it is a son, you shall kill him, but if it is a daughter, she shall live"* (Ex. 1:16). In other words, Shiphrah and Puah would represent Pharaoh's deadly hands in the delivery room, waiting to smother sons and God's promised offspring to Abraham. This was a vile task to assign to midwives. Yet how could they possibly refuse the king of Egypt? After all, he was meant to be feared, right?

The serpent enticed Eve with forbidden fruit to *"make her like God"* (Gen. 3:4–7). The first woman didn't fear God enough to resist the snake. Now a pharaoh, worshipped as a god, was offering two lowly women the authority to serve as *his* sole agents in his defense of Egypt. Pharaoh's words may have swayed Shiphrah and Puah had their hearts desired glory. *"But the midwives feared God and did not do as the king of Egypt commanded them, but let the male children live"* (Ex. 1:17). They defied Pharaoh. They feared God above a frightened king and their obedience displayed the wise reverence Eve lacked at the beginning. They were not deceived by the snake-king. Instead, they used the serpent's tool of deception against him.

The exact nature of their defiance isn't explained. When questioned about the many bouncing baby boys thriving in Israelite homes, they gave this report: *"Hebrew women are not like the Egyptian women, for they are vigorous and give birth before the midwife comes to them"* (Ex. 1:19). Was this statement a bold lie? Did Shiphrah and Puah attend each birth, catching, cleaning, and swaddling newborn boys, along with the girls? Or did they intentionally delay their services, perhaps popping in *after* Hebrew children were already delivered (Ex. 1:18–19)? The text doesn't say. But whatever they did, it was done in fear of a higher throne. God was pleased to bless them. He *"dealt well with the midwives ... God gave them families"* (Ex. 1:20–21). Shiphrah and Puah's account ends with the birth of *more* Israelite children – including their own. The irony of this cements the point of the passage: God's purposes cannot be thwarted.

Exodus 1 confirms God's covenant promise to Abraham. Israel multiplied despite the death of her patriarchs, her ruthless enslavement, and the plots of a serpentine pharaoh. The nation was sustained in the face of a threatening enemy and God used the fear and obedience of two humble women in his work of salvation. But isn't that how God works? In Shiphrah and Puah, we are reminded of the Man who saved his people from death – not by the might of the sword but – through his humble obedience (Phil. 2:5–8). Because of that man, Jesus, no amount of satanic enmity or persecution can frustrate God's purposes for his people today. Be encouraged! No matter the opposition, God's people persevere because the risen Christ sustains us.

11

Jochebed

Remember God's shelter amid the waters of death

(Exodus 2:1–10)

Reflection

Jochebed remembered God's former work of salvation in preserving her son. Christ fulfills this – and every Old Testament – picture of salvation.

The story of Moses' birth and adoption are told in Exodus 2:1–10. It's the second of a two-part drama. In Part 1 (Ex. 1), a crafty pharaoh attempted to use slavery and midwives to destroy Israel. He sought to kill God's people, but to no avail. The King of Heaven prevailed over the king of Egypt and the Israelites multiplied instead. But Pharaoh didn't give up. Exodus 1 closes with a dreadful order to his people: *"Every son that is born to the Hebrews you shall cast into the Nile, but you shall let every daughter live"* (Ex. 1:22). Enslavement and the local midwifery practice had failed him – but surely his own people wouldn't. Right? Moses' birth story answers this question.

The account begins in Exodus 2:1 with a nameless introduction of Moses' parents. Details come in Exodus 6:20. The family was from the line of Levi (Leah's third son). Moses' mother, Jochebed, was his father's aunt. The law would later forbid similar arrangements (Lev. 18:6, 12–14). But for now, the couple sat in the full throes of family life. Their eldest child was a daughter named Miriam (Ex. 2:4), followed by three-year-old Aaron (Ex. 7:7). Pharaoh's fatal law must have arrived sometime after the birth of Aaron since he was alive and didn't appear to be in danger of the edict. Unfortunately for Jochebed, her third pregnancy collided with the crisis of the decree. The king's war against a nation found its target in her womb.

Jochebed's pregnancy must have been an anxious one. Perhaps she kept the announcement *and* her bulging belly from neighbors. Maybe she prayed regularly for a daughter – and for courage, if otherwise. Whatever the case, her labor and delivery ended with a boy. A son in Israel was a gift to celebrate under normal circumstances. Members of the house of Levi would have rejoiced to see him. But a genocidal serpentine king was not a normal circumstance and so the baby was concealed. Exodus 2:2 says that *"When she saw that he was a fine child, she hid him three months."*

I'm caring for my two-month-old foster son as I write this chapter. The idea of "hiding him" seems impossible to me. A routine diaper change can trigger his cries to the neighbors for rescue. Newborns are noisy, needy people. Jochebed's ability to keep her boy under Pharaoh's radar testifies to her determination to preserve his life. She was surely motivated by love. But Exodus 2:2 suggests something more.

Jochebed saw that her son was a fine child (Ex. 2:2). Stephen, in the New Testament, interprets this verse as a child *"beautiful in God's sight"* (Acts 7:20). Perhaps Jochebed recognized the infant Moses as a future deliverer of God's people. Lamech, Noah's father, saw something similar in his son at birth. He said this: *"Out of the ground that the Lord has cursed, this one shall bring us relief from our work and from the painful toil of our hands"* (Gen. 5:29).

Noah's ark *had* brought salvation to his family and preserved humankind (Gen. 7:23). But the effects of the Fall remained. Jochebed felt the toil of her enslavement and bitter work. And she knew the biting reality of the Genesis 3:16 judgment poem to Woman: *"in pain you shall bring forth children."* In Jochebed's case, she bore a child sentenced to death. Where was God's promise of relief and blessing through seed and land (Gen. 3:15; 12:1–3)? Maybe the Lord would bring that deliverance through her beautiful son. She resolved to guard his life.

"When she could hide him no longer, she took for him a basket made of bulrushes and daubed it with bitumen and pitch. She put the child in it and placed it among the reeds by the riverbank" (Ex. 2:3). Jochebed appeared to be an Israelite with a good memory. When her son grew too large and too loud to hide, she recalled God's former work of salvation. She remembered Noah's ark. John L. Mackay writes in his Exodus commentary:

> *The word for "basket" is the same [here] as that used 28 times for Noah's ark (Gen. 6:14) and is only used elsewhere here and in verse 5. Clearly this basket was intended to be a means of conveying the young child to safety from threatening catastrophe – and who can doubt that it was constructed with a mother's prayers that it provide as effective a deliverance as Noah's ark had?*[1]

Jochebed considered the pattern of God's salvation in the days of Noah – God's ark had been the only means of safety through the waters of death. Did she repeat that story of deliverance as she daubed bulrushes with pitch? Did her lips quiver with prayers as she nursed her son by the finished basket? Did her heart pound within her as she set him in the Nile? In the end, she released her ark, giving her baby to the waters but ultimately to God.

In truth, God's name is never mentioned in Moses' birth story. Yet the irony of the baby's rescue boasts of God's redemptive purposes. It was he who ordered Jochebed's drifting ark into the hands of Pharaoh's daughter. The woman, moved with pity for the crying child, adopted him as her own. His watchful big sister, Miriam, intervened on behalf of her mother and Pharaoh's daughter employed a wet nurse to nourish and raise the boy until weaned. And so, the mother who, in faith, had laid her infant in the Nile, was paid with Pharaoh's money to receive him back (Ex. 2:5–10). The snake-king was defeated again – this time his own household played a hand.

Moses' birth story reminds us of someone else – a distant baby who was also delivered from the seed of the serpent. King Herod sought to kill Jesus at birth, but God preserved his life through the obedience of faithful parents (Mt. 2:13–23). Jesus lived to serve as our final deliverer, one greater than Moses (Heb. 3:1–6). Jesus is the promised Seed who will free us eternally from the painful effects of the curse. He alone is our shelter amid the waves of God's judgment, and we do well to remember our Savior. Jochebed's narrative affirms the wisdom of recalling God's work of salvation.

12

Zipporah

The mark of our family resemblance

(Exodus 2:11–25 and 4:18–31)

Reflection

God's diverse new covenant community gathers not to conform to one cultural expression of faith, but to live out their Spirit-enabled wholehearted devotion to the Savior.

Zipporah, Moses' wife, is mentioned three times by name in Scripture. She marries her husband in Exodus 2:21, she circumcises her son in 4:25, and joins Israel's wilderness journey in 18:2–5. Zipporah might also be the wife discriminated against in Numbers 12:1 – but this is less certain. The point is this: her cameos in Scripture are few but not insignificant. As we will see, Zipporah's role in the story of redemption reveals the God who defines his covenant community by his terms – and not by their cultural norms. Her tale begins with a runaway Moses.

Moses first met his wife by a well in the land of Midian. He arrived there as a fugitive. The boy adopted into Pharaoh's household didn't pledge allegiance to Egypt but identified as a son of Abraham (Heb. 11:24–27; Acts 7:27). Moses chose to side with the oppressed people of God and killed an Egyptian in defense of an Israelite. He, then, fled to Midian to escape Pharaoh's death threat (Ex. 2:11–15). His journey brought him to a well, where he looked up to find a group of women approaching with their animals (Ex. 2:15–16). Moses' next move will remind us of his forebears.

In the manner of his great-great-grandmother, Rebekah, and his great-grandfather, Jacob, Moses rescued the women and watered their flock (Gen. 24:11–19; 29:1–19). The group comprised the seven daughters of Reuel (also called Jethro), the priest of Midian (Ex. 3:1). One of them was Zipporah. She and her sisters had been the target of harassment. Local shepherds may have waited for these women to do the hard work of drawing water *before* driving them away to benefit from their labor.[1] The abuse was likely routine – consider Jethro's surprise at seeing his daughters home early in Exodus 2:18. Perhaps Zipporah walked to the well that day anticipating a long struggle. What she found instead was a man, dressed like an Egyptian, eager to intercede and save.

Zipporah's savior entered the family as her husband. She and Moses had two sons – Gershom and Eliezer (Ex. 2:21–22; 18:2–4). Moses tended the flocks of Jethro for the next forty years in the wilderness of Midian (Ex. 3:1).[2] Possibly, Zipporah saw nothing but a quiet Midianite life with her husband and sons. If so, imagine the shock of Exodus 3.

Moses returned from the mountain of Horeb with news: *Yahweh*, the God of Israel, had appeared to him. The cries of his enslaved people had reached his ears. He remembered his covenant with their fathers Abraham, Isaac, and Jacob. God was sending Moses to Pharoah to deliver the Israelites from slavery and to bring them to God's Promised Land (Ex. 3:7–10). Zipporah's familiar family life in Midian was over. *"So Moses took his wife and his sons and had them ride on a donkey, and went back to the land of Egypt"* (Ex. 4:20). Unusual happenings awaited Zipporah on this journey. Consider Exodus 4:24–26:

At a lodging place on the way the Lord met him and sought to put him to death. Then Zipporah took a flint and cut off her son's foreskin and touched Moses' feet with it and said, "Surely you are a bridegroom of blood to me!" So he let him alone. It was then that she said, "A bridegroom of blood," because of the circumcision.

This text is among the strangest and most ambiguous passages in Scripture. The Hebrew doesn't address a single male by a proper name, it only uses the pronoun "him." The name "Moses" in verse 25 is inserted by the ESV translators to provide some clarity. In other words, there are three men in these verses: Moses, and his sons Gershom and Eliezer. Which of these three was the Lord seeking to kill? Which of the two brothers was circumcised? And whose feet (possibly a euphemism for genitals) did Zipporah touch with the foreskin? The passage is peculiar, and we can't answer much without speculation – but this much we know: the circumcision of a son turned away the threat of death.

Many scholars believe that the initial "him" in the text is Moses.[3] He's the target of God's death threat. Pharaoh had sought to kill Moses at his escape from Egypt and now God sought to kill him at his return (Ex. 2:15). The crime wasn't manslaughter this time but covenant unfaithfulness. Circumcision was the sign of God's covenant with Abraham and his offspring. Every male in Israel was to carry a reminder of God's promises in his flesh and those who didn't were cut off as covenant-breakers (Gen. 17:9–14). Moses had fled Egypt as a son of Israel. Had the transpiring years conformed him to the ways of Midian? He was returning as Israel's covenant mediator – and yet his own son didn't resemble a seed of Abraham. Zipporah seemed to understand this somehow and took a flint knife in her hands.

We don't know how this mother felt about the practice of Israelite circumcision. Her *"bridegroom of blood"* statement suggests possible disdain. Had she argued against circumcision in the family? Did she prefer to raise her sons to be more "Midianite" than "Israelite"? Whatever her view,

Zipporah circumcised her son to reroute the angel of death – and in so doing, she presented a foreshadowing of the Passover.

The verses that precede her bloody act foretell the death of Egyptian firstborns (Ex. 4:22–23). God would later pass through the land to strike firstborn males in each home – both man and beast (Ex. 12:12). Israel would escape this judgment, not because of her righteousness but, by a sign of blood (Ex. 12:13). An unblemished lamb would take the place of her firstborn sons. In a similar way, God passed over Moses (and ultimately his sons) because of another covenant sign of blood – one applied by the hand of a fast-acting Zipporah.

Zipporah and her sons left Egypt for Midian sometime after this grisly episode. Moses sent them away, perhaps out of concern for their safety (Ex. 18:2–3). Zipporah may have been content to remain in her Midianite community – yet she returned with her sons to Moses. They joined Israel near Mount Sinai (Ex. 2:5). We can't say what Zipporah understood of *Yahweh*. We can only hope that she came to trust the God who marks his people by his work of salvation and not by their cultural preferences. *Yahweh's* plan from the beginning was to draw the families of the earth to himself through his redeemed people (Gen. 12:1–3; Ex. 9:16). God willing, the one who ultimately delivered Zipporah from harassing shepherds also called her to the Shepherd of Israel (Ps. 80:1).

Today, God gathers a new covenant community to himself – made up of countless tribes, tongues, and peoples (Rev. 7:9–10). We come not to conform to one cultural expression of faith, but to unite under the blood poured out for the forgiveness of our sins (Rev. 5:9–10). Our salvation is made evident by a true circumcision, not visible in the flesh but in the heart (Rom. 2:28–29). From South America to the Middle East, from Asia to West Africa (where I was born), God's true church is recognized by her Spirit-enabled, wholehearted devotion to the God of her salvation. May *Yahweh* find this mark of family resemblance on our hearts.

13

Miriam

The Lord has triumphed gloriously. Sing!

(Exodus 15 and Numbers 12)

Reflection

It wasn't the Egyptian state that kept Miriam from God's Promised Land – it was her own sin. Rejoice! The Promised One who heals us from sin has come!

Tradition identifies Miriam as the unnamed big sister of Exodus 2. She emerges early in that book as a resourceful rescuer – and later as a praising prophetess. But Miriam is also spotted in the book of Numbers, and there we meet her as an irreverent instigator (Num. 12). Miriam reminds us that God's salvation is more than national liberation. God's covenant people need freedom from both their physical oppression *and* their enslavement to sin.

Miriam, the daughter of Amram and Jochebed, was sister to three-year-old Aaron and an infant Moses (Ex. 2:1–2; 7:7). Scripture doesn't mention her age at the time of Pharaoh's death order against Hebrew newborn boys. We only know that she was old enough to understand the danger the law posed to her newest brother. Older sisters can be protective of younger siblings. I'm the mother of two daughters at elementary school and an infant foster son. My girls are captured by their little brother. It seems there's nothing they wouldn't do to soothe his whines and win his smiles. I wonder if this was Miriam with baby Moses. Perhaps Miriam was Jochebed's best assistant in the three months that Moses was concealed from neighbors (Ex. 2:2). Likely she was at hand as her brother was placed in a basket and set loose on the Nile. If so, her resolution in Exodus 2:4 makes sense: *"And his sister stood at a distance to know what would be done to him."*

Miriam watched the basket come into the hands of Pharaoh's daughter. She heard the princess recognize her brother as a Hebrew. She noticed her pity for him (Ex. 2:5–6). She spoke: *"Shall I go and call you a nurse from the Hebrew women to nurse the child for you?"* (Ex. 2:7). The Egyptian consented and Miriam's wise intercession ensured Moses' return to his Hebrew home. He would live openly with Amram and Jochebed until weaned – possibly three years. Those formative months must have sealed Moses' identity as an offspring of Abraham (Ex. 2:11). His adoption and education in Pharaoh's court didn't confuse his later call to serve as a covenant mediator between *Yahweh* and Israel (Acts 7:22; Ex. 3:7–10). By the end of Exodus 14, God had used Miriam's baby brother to redeem the Israelites from their Egyptian bondage – and Miriam sings of the victory in Exodus 15.

Her name is mentioned for the first time in that chapter. She's introduced as *"Miriam the prophetess, the sister of Aaron"* (Ex. 15:20). She's the first female prophet listed in Scripture. The precocious girl of Exodus 2 became influential in Israel. Miriam took a tambourine in her hand by the Red Sea and all the women followed her with dancing and instruments. She lifted her voice and directed them in a song that boasted of God's defeat of Egypt (Ex. 15:21).

Exodus 15 has two songs that read like a soundtrack to the narrative.

The first is sung by Moses and Israel (Ex. 15:1–19). The words remember God's judgments over Egypt (15:1–12); foretell the coming conquest of Canaan (15:13–18); and recall the parting of the Red Sea and Pharaoh's drowned army (15:19). Altogether, this first track is the unabashed praise of a triumphant God. No credit is assigned to Moses or any other leader. Israel's past salvation and future settlement rest on her glorious God. The second song is a refrain that echoes the first (Ex. 15:21).[1] It was sung by Miriam over the woman. Unfortunately, her tune would change in the book of Numbers. Miriam's envy and ego overshadowed her view of *Yahweh,* the conquering warrior.

The sister who helped to preserve her baby brother, now conspired to oppose him. Numbers 12:1 identifies Aaron in the ploy, but the order of names and the use of a feminine verb in the Hebrew suggests Miriam as the instigator.[2] Israel's leading lady wanted more spotlight. So, she used Moses' marriage to a foreigner to veil her envy and question his authority.[3] *"Has the Lord indeed spoken only through Moses? Has he not spoken through us also?"* (Num. 12:2). The questions appeared true on the surface. After all, God *had* used all three siblings in the Exodus (Mic. 6:4). But God heard the words and came down. He saw behind the mask and his anger burned (Num. 12:5–8).

Moses was commissioned to lead God's household as *his* servant. He was a prophet like none other, one who beheld the very form of the Lord (Num. 12:6–7). To dispute Moses' position was to doubt *Yahweh*'s sovereign choice. The root of Miriam and Aaron's crime was exposed by God's interrogation: *"Why then were you not afraid to speak against my servant Moses?"* (Num. 12:8). The siblings had acted without fearing God. So, *Yahweh* struck prophetess Miriam with leprosy (Num. 12:10). The conqueror of Egypt was also the judge of Israel.

Leprosy is known as Hansen's disease today. It's the result of an infectious bacteria that attacks the nerves under the skin, causing a loss of sensation and possible paralysis or disfigurement.[4] We can't name Miriam's illness as Hansen's since the word "leprosy" in Hebrew includes various skin conditions.[5] But whatever her case, it was serious. Aaron described her *"as one dead, whose flesh is half eaten away when he comes out of his mother's womb"* (Num. 12:10–12). Moses interceded for his stricken big sister and God healed and restored Miriam after seven days (Num. 12:13–16). Her skin disease was gone but she would never see the Promised Land. And neither would the generation that danced and sang by the Red Sea. Miriam's rebellion was only one of several in Numbers.

A tabernacle had been constructed for *Yahweh* in the wilderness (Ex. 35:4 – 40:38). He covenanted with Israel and dwelt among them like a father preparing his children for a journey (Ex. 19:5–6). God counted Israel (Num. 1); he arranged the tribes into traveling groups (Num. 2); he called the Levites for special duties (Num. 3 – 4); and made provision for purity and worship (Num. 5 – 10). The cloud representing his presence lifted over the tabernacle and Israel began her journey toward the Promised Land (Num. 10:11–12). The Abrahamic blessing of land was in view (Gen. 12:1–3). And then a cycle of sin began between Numbers 11 and 14. Miriam's was one, and the final was Israel's refusal to enter Canaan at the dispiriting report of ten spies (Num. 13:25 – 14:4). Once more, God heard and judged. Miriam and her generation (except for Caleb and Joshua, the faithful spies) would perish in the desert (Num. 14:20–38). She died in the wilderness of Zin and was buried there (Num. 20:1).

In Miriam, we see that ruthless Pharoah wasn't Israel's ultimate enemy. It wasn't the force of the Egyptian state that kept her from God's Promised Land. It was her own sin. We can disparage leprous Miriam, or we can recognize her leprosy as a picture of our own sin. Some of us experience insidious dissatisfaction, paralyzing envy, and a love for recognition that can desensitize our fear of God. We need grace to approach the One who heals us from sin. We must pray with the leper in Matthew 8:1–4: *"Lord, if you will, you can make me clean."* Christ, the promised Savior, is willing. He has triumphed to deliver his church from the disease of sin – and that's something we can sing about!

As we move on to study women in the time of the conquest and the judges in Part Four of the book, we will hear Deborah and Hannah bellow their own praises in song – just as Miriam once sang.

PART FOUR:

Women of the Conquest and the Time of the Judges

14

Rahab

The saving faith of a Canaanite prostitute

(Joshua 2 and 6:15–27)

Reflection

A prostitute with eyes as blind as her gods learned of Yahweh's acts of salvation and judgment, and she was enabled to see the Lord of heaven and earth. Salvation belongs to God alone.

A movie version of Joshua 2 would need a flashback scene at verse 1. The conquest of Canaan was at hand and Joshua was sending men on a reconnaissance mission. But Israel had been in this position before. Moses had made the same move about forty years earlier. Our contextual flashback takes us to Numbers 13 – 14.

Moses sent twelve spies, including Joshua, to survey Canaan (Num. 13:1–16). These men must have been careful scouts because they managed to explore for forty days without detection. They returned to Moses carrying fruits and news: "*We came to the land which you sent us. It flows with milk and honey, and this is its fruit. However, the people who dwell in the land are strong, and the cities are fortified and very large ... We are not able to go up against the people, for they are stronger than we are"* (Num. 13:27–31). The spies, apart from Joshua and Caleb, gave a discouraging report. And Israel trusted these incredulous men over *Yahweh*.

Israelites who had witnessed God's conquering power in Egypt, refused to enter the Promised Land at the counsel of ten spies (Num. 13:25–33). For this, God promised death: *"none of the men who have seen my glory and my signs that I did in Egypt and in the wilderness ... shall see the land that I swore to give to their father ... except Caleb the son of Jephunneh and Joshua the son of Nun"* (Num. 14:22–30). For four decades, mothers and fathers dropped like flies in the desert. Moses' dead body was the last to fall and Joshua became Israel's new leader (Deut. 34; Josh. 1:1–2). Joshua prepared to cross the Jordan River into the Promised Land with a young nation that had not even witnessed the events of the Exodus. Would they trust *Yahweh* when their parents hadn't?

Our flashback returns us to Joshua 2:1 with more tension than when we left. We hear Joshua commanding two men to go and scan the land. What message would they bring back? Would the report of *these* scouts nurture faith or doubt?

The men entered the city of Jericho and found cover in the home of a prostitute named Rahab (Josh. 2:1). Unfortunately for Joshua, his spies proved more conspicuous than the first group back in Numbers 13. His agents are outed to the king of Jericho by verse 2 and pinned at Rahab's house by verse 3. Rahab was subpoenaed: *"Bring out the men who have come to you, who entered your house, for they have come to search out all the land"* (Josh. 2:3). The spies were at the mercy of this Canaanite woman. Surely, Joshua's first operation as Israel's general was coming to a fast and demoralizing end. And then we read verse 4 and its shocking statement: *"But the woman had taken the two men and hidden them"* (Josh. 2:4).

Rahab was siding with the enemy! She hid the Israelites under stalks of flax on her roof and lied: *"True, the men came to me, but I did not know where they were from. And when the gate was about to be closed at dark, the men went out. I do not know where the men went. Pursue them quickly, for you will overtake them"* (Josh. 2:4–5). Rahab must have held a good poker face because the guards never doubted her. They sped off into the night and the city gates were shut behind them, leaving the spies on her roof (Josh. 2:6–7). The concealed Israelites were left to wonder why a Canaanite prostitute would shield Hebrew invaders.

Rahab crept to the roof that night to explain herself. She said that Jericho was melting with fear because *Yahweh* was giving Canaan to Israel (Josh. 2:8–9). She based her certainty of this on God's manifested power in the Exodus and wilderness: *"For we have heard how the Lord dried up the water of the Red Sea before you when you came out of Egypt, and what you did to the two kings of the Amorites who were beyond the Jordan, to Sihon and Og, whom you devoted to destruction"* (Josh. 2:10). Israel's older generation had seen what Rahab had only heard about. They had doubted God and revolted, yet she believed and protected his people. Her next words should have put them to shame: *"for the Lord your God, he is God in the heavens above and on the earth beneath"* (Josh. 2:11). In this Canaanite woman, we see that the Exodus was meant to ransom Israel *and* awaken faith among the families of the earth.

God told Pharaoh back in Exodus 9:16: *"for this purpose I have raised you up, to show you my power, so that my name may be proclaimed in all the earth."* Somewhere in Jericho, a pagan prostitute learned of *Yahweh*'s acts of salvation and judgment and was enabled to believe that Israel's God was the Lord of heaven and earth. Now the Lord was using her testimony to strengthen Joshua and a young Israel. Rahab offered directions to the spies and they escaped to their camp after three days (Josh. 2:16, 22–23). Their report to Joshua was almost a verbatim quote of Rahab: *"Truly the Lord has given all the land into our hands. And also, all the inhabitants of the land melt away because of us"* (Josh. 2:24). God used an unlikely voice to reassure his people. Joshua and Israel would cross the Jordan to conquer a land their parents never saw.

The narrative seems to end well. Rahab and her family were spared from death in exchange for her preservation of the spies (Josh. 2:14–16; 6:22–23). We could end our study here – but for one question: what are we to think of Rahab's lie? Lying is a sin (Ex. 20:16), and still it appears as if Rahab was saved from God's judgment because of her deceitful tactics. Should we smile over her ruse, or frown?

The narrator of the story doesn't affirm or criticize Rahab's actions. Analysis waits for the New Testament and there we read: *"By faith Rahab the prostitute did not perish with those who were disobedient, because she had given a friendly welcome to the spies"* (Heb. 11:31). According to Hebrews, Rahab wasn't saved because of her deception, but through the instrument by which all are saved, faith. James adds this: *"was not also Rahab the prostitute justified by works when she received the messengers and sent them out by another way?"* (Jas. 2:25). James interprets Rahab's protection of the spies as *evidence* of her saving faith. In other words – like the Hebrew midwives of Exodus 1 or the ten Boom family in 1940 Nazi-occupied Netherlands – Rahab subverted local authorities at the risk of her own life because of her faith in a greater authority (Acts 4:19–20).

This lying prostitute doesn't offer much beyond her faith. And this reminds us: we're not justified by our virtues, but by God's gift of faith *alone*. The only work that can justify us is Jesus' perfect obedience. Yet those saved by faith, are also enabled by the Spirit to yield the fruits of faith.[1] We see this in Rahab. A movie version of her story might begin with a flashback *and* end with a flashforward. This latter scene would picture the Canaanite being weaved into the fabric of Israel's history as ancestor to a son named Boaz, who is also ancestor to Christ, the sinless Seed (Mt. 1:5–6; Josh. 6:25). Rahab's film might close with praises to the God who reveals his grace through *"vessels of mercy, which he has prepared beforehand for glory ... not from the Jews only but also from the Gentiles"* (Rom. 9:22–24).

15

Deborah and Jael

Women given to the Savior's cause

(Judges 4 – 5)

Reflection

God's purposes in salvation will always advance – even through unexpected people.

Deborah and Jael's narrative reminds me of a hand-drawn sketch in pencil. There are shadings and shadows in the story that make the light more brilliant. By this light, we see the God who uses unlikely people in his work of salvation. This God built a nation through weak matriarchs in Genesis. He enabled the women of the Exodus to save lives. And in Judges 4, he called a singing judge and a tent-dwelling wife to deliver Israel from her enemies.

The narrative is set in the years following Joshua's death. He had crossed the Jordan River with Israel into the Promised Land. The people served *Yahweh* all the days of Joshua's life (Judg. 2:7). But a generation rose after his passing who didn't know the Lord or his works.

They abandoned the God of their fathers for the gods of Canaan (Judg. 2:10–12). *"So the anger of the* L*ORD was kindled against Israel, and he gave them over to plunderers, who plundered them"* (Judg. 2:14). The land of milk and honey became a place of thorns and thistles for God's covenant people (Judg. 2:3; Gen. 3:17–18). Clearly, Israel's peace was found in her obedience to *Yahweh* rather than her possession of land.

God's people cried out and he showed pity. *Yahweh* elected and empowered judges to defeat Israel's enemies. *"But whenever the judge died, they turned back and were more corrupt than their fathers, going after other gods, serving them and bowing down to them"* (Judg. 2:19). Israel would provoke God's anger and he would again strengthen her adversaries against her. This pattern of apostasy, judgment, groaning, repentance, and gracious salvation cycles throughout the book of Judges. And it's here we find Deborah, Israel's fourth judge.

Deborah – Scripture's second prophetess and sole female judge – came to power in dire times (Judg. 4:4). God had turned his people over to Jabin, the king of Canaan. The commander of Jabin's army was Sisera, a fierce military leader with a fleet of 900 chariots of iron. The force of these vehicles gave Sisera an advantage and he *"oppressed the people of Israel cruelly for twenty years"* (Judg. 4:1–3). To make matters worse, Israelite leaders seemed unwilling to rise, resist, and complete the conquest of the land first promised to Abraham their father.

God told Abraham back in Genesis 15:16 that his offspring would displace the Amorites as judgment against their sin. God's plan was to display his justice through his covenant people. But idolatry distracted the Israelites and, instead of driving out the inhabitants, they nestled down among them (Judg. 1:27–36). It seems Israel was especially inactive in the days of Deborah. She sings later in Judges 5 to commend the warriors *"who offered themselves willingly"* to God's cause (Judg. 5:2, 9). She also condemns the many who sat and did nothing (Judg. 5:12–18, 23, 24). In fact, many commentaries link Deborah's judgeship to the apparent indifference of men in her day.[1] God raised up a *"mother in*

Israel" at a time of external oppression and internal passivity (Judg. 5:7).

Deborah used to sit under a palm tree in the hill country of Ephraim "*and the people of Israel came up to her for judgment*" (Judg. 4:5). Like a true momma settling clashes between her children, she resolved disputes among God's people. But she didn't just hear public cases, she also gave private commands in the office of a prophetess. Deborah charged Barak, a military general from the tribe of Naphtali, with these words: "*Has not the LORD, the God of Israel, commanded you, 'Go, gather your men at Mount Tabor, taking 10,000 from the people of Naphtali and the people of Zebulun'?*" (Judg. 4:6). Israel's cries had stirred God's mercy (Judg. 4:3). He was ready to strike Sisera at the Kishon River and hand him over to Israel (Judg. 4:6–7). Barak needed to believe and obey. But faithless apathy was high in Israel, so Naphtali's general refused to act without "Israel's mother" at his side. He told Deborah: "*If you will go with me, I will go, but if you will not go with me, I will not go*" (Judg. 4:8). She agreed to accompany him into battle. But the glory, she said, would belong to a woman, not to him (Judg. 4:9).

The reader is left to imagine Deborah as this anticipated glorious woman. She's heard prodding Barak at the battle: "*Up! For this is the day in which the LORD has given Sisera into your hand. Does not the LORD go out before you?*" (Judg. 4:14). And indeed, the fight belonged to the Lord. For he "*routed Sisera and all his chariots and all his army before Barak by the edge of the sword*" (Judg. 4:15). The word "routed" (*hamam* in Hebrew) is the same used to describe the panic that sank Pharaoh's chariots in the Red Sea (Ex. 14:24).[2] God sent a storm to flood the Kishon River and it engulfed Sisera's chariots (Judg. 5:4). *Yahweh* replayed his former work of salvation for a generation who didn't know his feats. Every Canaanite soldier died but Sisera. He scurried away on foot and Barak pursued to kill (Judg. 4:15–16).

It's here that we meet Jael. She's introduced as the wife of Heber the Kenite (Judg. 4:17). The Kenites were the descendants of Moses' father-in-law – Zipporah's people. They had served as guides for Israel in the wilderness and had settled with the tribe of Judah in the Promised Land (Num. 10:29–32; Judg. 1:16). But for some reason, Jael's husband had pitched his tent away from his people and was friendly with Israel's enemies (Judg. 4:17). Sisera felt free to seek refuge in Jael's tent – and she encouraged him with warm words, warm milk, and a warm blanket (Judg. 4:18–19). The reader never doubts Jael's loyalty to the fugitive until verse 21. *"But Jael the wife of Heber took a tent peg, and took a hammer in her hand. Then she went softly to him and drove the peg into his temple until it went down into the ground while he was lying fast asleep from weariness. So he died"* (Judg. 4:21). She killed Sisera – Israel's cruel twenty-year tyrant – and led Barak to his dead body (Judg. 4:22).

Heber had migrated away from his people but apparently, Jael's heart had remained with the Kenites – Israel's allies. Her stunning break from hospitality recalls Rahab in some ways: the Canaanite prostitute had deceived her nation to shelter Israelite spies (Josh. 2:4–5). In reverse, this Kenite wife violated ancient Near Eastern hospitality (and her husband's association with King Jabin) to defeat Israel's foe. The result in both cases was the destruction of oppressive nations God had sentenced to judgment (Josh. 6:17, Judg. 4:23–24).[3] Jael's method was questionable – nevertheless, she emerged in the story as the victorious woman of verse 9. The New Testament doesn't assign faith to her in the way it does to Rahab – yet Deborah blessed Jael in a song that seemed to anticipate God's promised Seed:

> *Most blessed of women be Jael ... of tent-dwelling women most blessed ... she struck Sisera; she crushed his head; she shattered and pierced his temple. Between her feet he sank, he fell, he lay still; between her feet he sank, he fell; where he sank, there he fell – dead* (Judg. 5:24–27).

Deborah's repeated words paint the image of an enemy, head crushed, dead at the feet of a victor. Her lyrics here sound a lot like Genesis 3:15. That earlier poem promised enmity between the Seed of the Woman and the seed of the serpent. The snake would bruise the Savior's heel, but he would crush his head. The ancient serpent would sink and fall dead at his feet. Jael had shattered Sisera, bringing forty years of peace to Israel (Judg. 5:31). Christ would crush the snake and all effects of the curse, leaving only eternal blessings (Rev. 21:1–4). The God who uses unexpected people in his story of redemption, was pleased to use two willing women to point to his promised Savior. Blessed is every woman who offers herself fully to that Savior's cause.

16

The Levite's Concubine

The concubine, the crime, and the king

(Judges 19)

Reflection

God's Genesis 3:15 promise of salvation seems distant in Judges 19, and it often seems far from our dark world. Still, Yahweh's promises will always prove faithful – even when we're not.

There's a legendary crime case discussed in many undergraduate psychology programs (I've heard it taught). Kitty Genovese was raped, robbed, and repeatedly stabbed outside her Queens, New York apartment building in 1964. The killing was horrific, but it's not mentioned in Psych 101 courses for its gruesomeness. Professors don't generally focus on Genovese or her murderer – but on the bystanders. It was reported that several neighbors heard her screams for help but didn't act to save her life. Their supposed indifference is explained by a social theory known as the "bystander effect." This states that a bystander is less likely to assist someone if in a group than if they are alone. I share Genovese's case to make a point: the tragic murder of one young woman led to the social psychological diagnosis of an entire people.

Something similar takes place in Judges 19. The narrator captures the societal degeneration of Israel through the murder story of one Levite's concubine.

The cycle of apostasy, judgment, and rescue, noted at the start of Judges, spirals downward as the book continues. Israel persisted to forsake her God and the temporal salvation of her human judges proved insufficient. In fact, many of the judges we meet after Deborah struggle with personal faithfulness themselves. For instance, Gideon tempted the nation to idolatry by propping up a golden ephod that some worshiped (Judg. 8:22–28). Abimelech, Gideon's son, killed his seventy brothers on one stone (Judg. 9:5). Jephthah made a rash oath that he believed obliged him to an unlawful child sacrifice (Judg. 11:29–40). And what can we say about the unrestrained Samson, who tossed away his vows and life chasing Philistine women (Judg. 14 – 16)? Israelite society goes from bad to worse by the end of Judges.

In fact, our narrator seems to give up on the idea of judges altogether after Samson. The author perceives a need for a righteous king and concludes the book with a couple of stories that convey the madness of an apostate Israel without this king. His repeated refrain in Chapters 17 – 21 is this: *"In those days there was no king in Israel. Everyone did what was right in his own eyes"* (17:6; 18:1; 19:1; 21:25). The death of the Levite's concubine in Judges 19 is among these tales and it could win a prize for the number of laws broken in one narrative. Just consider the first verse alone.

It begins like this: *"a certain Levite was sojourning in the remote parts of the hill country of Ephraim, who took to himself a concubine from Bethlehem in Judah"* (Judg. 19:1). This verse may sound like a typical marriage until you consider the identity of the characters. This man was a Levite. God had drawn the family of Levi to himself as priests and had given Moses detailed laws concerning their holiness. These included laws on marriage. A Levite was to *"take as his wife a virgin of his own people ... that he may not profane his offspring among his people"* (Lev. 21:13–15). The directness of the law doesn't seem to permit a concubine, who were often maidservants treated as mistresses with lower statuses (Gen. 16:1–2).[1] But crooked people shape wayward times, so an unnamed Levite married his unnamed concubine.

The questionable union was further compromised by adultery on the part of the concubine (Judg. 19:2). The passage says little about this woman beyond her infidelity and her hometown, Bethlehem. We don't know the nature of her relationship with the Levite or the circumstances that landed her in the bed of another man. We only know that, according to the Mosaic law, she *and* the man who slept with her were to die (Deut. 22:22). If no evidence existed for death, God's law provided a test to either clear the innocent wife of all suspicion or leave the guilty woman to God's own judgment (Num. 5:11–31).[2] The purpose of these laws was to distinguish Israel as a holy people, separated to dwell with her covenant God (Lev. 20:22–26). Levites were to serve according to God's Word – this one treated his own sins, and those of his concubine's, with seeming indifference. He rode off to Bethlehem to reclaim his unfaithful and estranged mistress with the aim of speaking to her *"kindly"* (Judg. 19:3).

The Levite had planned a short visit to Bethlehem – but his father-in-law pressed him to stay longer (Judg. 19:4–9). The older man detained him with food and drink through the afternoon of the fifth day. He urged the Levite to remain until the sixth morning, *"But the man would not spend the night"* (Judg. 19:10). Anxious to be on his way, the Levite, with his servant and now reconciled concubine, traveled through the evening. He avoided foreign cities in hopes of finding shelter among Israelites in Gibeah – a town belonging to the tribe of Benjamin (Judg. 19:11–14). He must have expected the kind of welcome a Levite might get in Ephraim (Judg. 17:8–13). Unfortunately for him, Gibeah wasn't as willing. No one offered him room but an old Ephraimite sojourning there (Judg. 19:16). The party of three went home with the old man and the problem of lodging seemed solved until a sudden plot twist. Gibeah, a city comprising God's covenant people, had become the new Sodom. Rapists encircled the house.

Judges 19:22 reads: *"As they were making their hearts merry, behold, the men of the city, worthless fellows, surrounded the house, beating on the door. And they said to the old man, the master of the house, 'Bring out the man who came into your house, that we may know him.'"* The men of Gibeah demanded the Levite for sex and the old Ephraimite interceded to stop them according to the ancient Near Eastern law of hospitality (Judg. 19:23). The dialogue here is nearly identical to the one between Lot (Abraham's nephew) and the Sodomites in Genesis 19:4–9. Like Lot, the old man was willing to risk his own family for the protection of his guests – but only his male guests. The next scene of the narrative reveals the danger an anarchic society can be to vulnerable women. The old Ephraimite offered his daughter and the concubine to the group and the Levite seized and flung the latter woman outside (Judg. 19:24–25). The violent mob had come for him, he preserved himself by throwing his "wife" to them.

"And they knew her and abused her all night until the morning. And as the dawn began to break, they let her go. And as morning appeared, the woman came and fell down at the door of the man's house where her master was, until it was light" (Judg. 19:25–26). The woman in this narrative is nameless and speechless. We don't hear a word from her. Like Kitty Genovese, her screams in the night seemed silent. The Levite found her at the door in the morning and commanded her to rise – but she remained quiet (Judg. 19:28). Did she die by that door? The specific moment of her death is unclear (Judg. 20:5). We only know that the Levite carried her home by donkey to divide her body limb by limb into twelve pieces – one for each tribe in Israel (Judg. 19:29–30). He used the body parts of the silent woman to voice his complaint against Gibeah – and the people listened to him. The nation waged a civil war against the Benjaminites

and it ended in the abuse of even more women (Judg. 21 – 22). The narrator's point is clear: Israel was as vile as the Canaanites they had been redeemed to disposes. They broke the covenant God had made with them through Moses, so he sent the *"curses, confusion, and frustration"* promised for their evil (Deut. 28:20; Ex. 19:5).

The brutal killing of the Levite's concubine – like those in our day – screams out for a deliverer king. And Jesus Christ is that King. His righteousness is a safeguard for the powerless and his justice is perfect. He's a king who hears and sees the vulnerable. He sought out a woman – one trapped by sin and without standing in her community – and made her a renewed herald of good news (Jn. 4:4–26). God's Genesis 3:15 promise of salvation seems distant in Judges 19, and it often seems far from our dark world. Still, *Yahweh*'s promises will always prove faithful – even when we're not. So, lift your voice and testify of him in the darkness. And cry out in prayer to the One who listens, asking for the light of his kingdom to shine through his church today – and for his soon return.

17

Naomi

God's sovereign hand is good – in joy and in sorrow

(Ruth 1 – 4)

Reflection

The hand that emptied Naomi in Chapter 1, puts praise in her mouth by the end of Chapter 2. God is both perfectly loving and powerfully in control in times of grief.

The book of Ruth takes place in the time of the judges (Ruth 1:1). In it, we see that the tale of the Levite's concubine isn't the only story of a vulnerable woman in that era. The author of Ruth introduces us to two childless and impoverished widows who must persevere to survive in perilous days. The younger, a Moabite named Ruth, found refuge under the wings of *Yahweh* (Ruth 2:12). And the elder, an Israelite named Naomi, struggled with bitterness before seeing the generous hand of the God who orchestrates good purposes, even in treacherous times.

In many ways, the book of Ruth begins and ends with a focus on Naomi. Chapter 1 gives particular attention to her bereavement.

Famine uprooted her family from its native Bethlehem to foreign Moab. This famine in the period of the judges shouldn't surprise us. God had warned Israel of drought in the event of covenant unfaithfulness (Deut. 28:22–24). Still, the nation abandoned *Yahweh* and felt the emptiness of idolatry in her physical hunger. Bethlehem (translated as "the house of bread") became a place of scarcity. Elimelech, Naomi's husband, moved his wife and sons, Mahlon and Chilion, away from the Promised Land and their God-given inheritance (Ruth 1:1–2).

The family lingered in Moab and the stay brought a drought of the worst kind. Death stole the company of Elimelech, leaving Naomi alone with two sons (Ruth 1:3). The boys grew and married Moabite wives, *"the name of the one was Orpah and the name of the other Ruth. They lived there about ten years, and both Mahlon and Chilion died, so that the woman was left without her two sons and her husband"* (Ruth 1:4–5). Naomi, the once pleasant wife of Elimelech was reduced to a childless widow. Like a tree stripped of its fruit, she was without husband, sons, or joy. But she wasn't completely alone.

Naomi *"heard in the fields of Moab that the Lord had visited his people and given them food"* (Ruth 1:6). The God who brought the famine also granted rain. Naomi set out for home and her two daughters-in-law prepared to journey with her. At this point, the narrator permits Naomi a speech appealing to the young widows: *"Go, return each of you to her mother's house. May the Lord deal kindly with you, as you have dealt with the dead and with me. The Lord grant that you may find rest, each of you in the house of her husband!"* (Ruth 1:8–9). We see some of Naomi's faith and care in these words.

First, she prayed openly to *Yahweh* for her Moabite in-laws. She didn't invoke Baal or Chemosh (Canaanite deities) for the sake of their culture, but sought the living God of Israel for their security. Secondly, she prioritized their future over her immediate care by releasing them from all obligations to herself. Ruth (and perhaps Oprah) must have caught a glimpse of *Yahweh's* covenant loving kindness (*hesed*) in

Naomi's sincere compassion for them over the years.[1] Ruth clung to the old woman and refused to return with her sister-in-law to the gods of Moab (Ruth 1:15–18). In the end, God would make this converted Moabite woman a gift to Naomi – even if she couldn't see it then. The two headed toward Bethlehem.

The town was roused by their arrival. The women gathered around the older woman and wondered, *"Is this Naomi?"* (Ruth 1:19). The cutting hand of suffering had left its mark on the widow and the scars were visible. She responded: *"Do not call me Naomi; call me Mara, for the Almighty has dealt very bitterly with me. I went away full, and the LORD has brought me back empty. Why call me Naomi, when the LORD has testified against me and the Almighty has brought calamity upon me?"* (Ruth 1:19–21). Naomi, meaning "sweet," had returned as Mara, meaning "bitter." The embittered widow had no husband or son to tend to her in a culture that tied her sustenance to their inheritance. The famine was over, but her hunger would remain because God had sent her back empty. Naomi didn't credit her circumstances to chance but to God. Her suffering wasn't a bout of bad luck, but his doing.

I've often considered Naomi "the female Job" of the Bible. She and Job could have been understanding friends. They both knew pain and loss (Job 1:13–21). And they both attributed their suffering to God's sovereign hand (Job 6:4). Like Job, Naomi's narrative inspires an old question: can a loving and all-powerful God ordain human suffering and remain wholly consistent with his character? Our passage answers "yes" as we continue.

The hand that emptied Naomi, in Chapter 1, now puts praise in her mouth by the end of Chapter 2. She and Ruth had arrived in Bethlehem at the start of the barley harvest (Ruth 1:22). The younger widow volunteered to be the breadwinner for the family and ventured onto unknown fields to collect leftover grain. Her feet *"happened to come to the part of the field belonging to Boaz"* (Ruth 2:3). The man was a "redeemer" – a close relative who, by Mosaic law, could marry a widow in the clan of

Elimelech, thus providing for the woman and producing an offspring to maintain the name of the dead with his property (Ruth 4:10). Naomi recognized God's providence in Ruth's footsteps and blessed him for his *hesed* (Ruth 2:19–20).

Naomi's empty arms are filled with a bouncing baby by the end of the narrative (Ruth 4:13–17). The child, a son of Boaz and Ruth, was Elimelech's heir by law. The women of the town named him Obed (meaning "servant") because he would grow to serve his grandmother in her old age (Ruth 4:17).[2] God gave a desolate woman joy and provision in the unsteady days of the judges. Yet, the closing verses of Ruth suggest a purpose beyond Naomi's temporal care. God was sending an ultimate Redeemer in the person of Jesus Christ – the son of Boaz, the son of Obed, the son of Jesse, and the ancestral son of King David (Ruth 4:18–22; Mt. 1:5). This Jesus would be the true servant who would suffer our griefs and the calamity brought by the judgment of our sin (Is. 53:3–4). In him we see God's perfect *hesed* to his fallen people.

God is both perfectly loving and powerfully in control in times of grief. He directs the universe and allows both tribulation and joy without ever sinning or overlooking human responsibility. The intricacies of this are a mystery we can't always understand. But we can trust ourselves to God's sovereign hand – whether in joy or in sorrow – and know that his purposes for those in Christ are good.

18

Ruth

Obedience above ancestry

(Ruth 1 – 4)

Reflection

God used a Moabite – one who did right in his eyes – to generate kings for wayward Israel and continue the line to his promised Seed. He honors obedience above lineage.

Many of us have examples of dysfunctionality somewhere in our family tree. We could tell tales of conflict and gross misbehavior among current or long-ago relatives. Whatever our stories, few could match Ruth's. The Moabites came from the incestuous union of Lot and his eldest daughter. The story is told in Genesis 19:30–38.

God had rained sulfur on Sodom, Lot's residence. He warned Lot's family to escape without hesitation: *"Do not look back or stop anywhere"* (Gen. 19:17). But Lot's wife disobeyed, she turned and became a pillar of salt (Gen. 19:26). Lot was frightened and went into the hills where he lived in a cave with his two daughters. The older daughter advised the younger, "*Our father is old, and there is not a man on earth to come in to us after the manner of all the earth. Come, let us make our father drink wine, and we will lie with him, that we may preserve offspring from our father*" (Gen. 19:31–32). Lust wasn't the main motivation, but a desire to preserve Lot's seed. So the daughters, likely influenced by the deviant sexual practices of Sodom, both became pregnant by their drunken father (Gen. 19:34–37). The eldest named her son Moab – the father of Ruth's people.

The Mosaic law forbade marriage to non-Israelites like Ruth (Deut. 7:1–4) because of the possibility of an Israelite husband turning to idols. The Moabites were infamous for this very thing. On the advice of a greedy diviner named Balaam, the people of Moab had sent women to seduce Israelite men in the wilderness. These men abandoned *Yahweh* for the Canaanite deity, Baal (Num. 25:1–9; 31:16). God's righteous anger brought judgment on both Israel and Moab. A plague killed 24,000 Israelites (Num. 25:9) and God cursed the Moabites, excluding them by name from his covenant community (Deut. 23:3–4). All this must have hung somewhere in the air as Mahlon, an Israelite man, noticed a Moabite woman named Ruth.

Famine had brought Mahlon's family (his father Elimelech, his mother Naomi, and brother Chilion) from their native Bethlehem of Judah to Moab. They came looking for food but were met by adversity. Elimelech died, leaving his wife and sons in a foreign land. Both boys grew up to marry Moabites – Mahlon married Ruth and Chilion married Orpah. Perhaps their dead father's departure from the Promised Land justified their decisions to take foreign brides. Whatever the case, the sons married without regard for the law. But then again, these were the kingless days of the judges, when everyone did what seemed right in their own eyes (Judg. 21:25; Ruth 1:1).

Shockingly, as the story continues, the author will depict a Moabite doing right in God's eyes.

Mahlon and Chilion died after ten years of marriage, leaving their wives widowed and childless. Emptied of everything but her two daughters-in-law, Naomi, rose to return to her country (Ruth 1:1–6). Ruth and Orpah began the journey with her but were soon urged to return. Naomi reasoned with them: a second marriage was more probable in their motherland than with a bereaved and bitter mother-in-law (Ruth 1:8–13). Orpah agreed – but Ruth didn't. The Moabite who should have pulled the family toward Baal had been drawn to the God of Israel. She clung to Naomi (and to *Yahweh)* with these words: *"Do not urge me to leave you or to return from following you. For where you go I will go, and where you lodge I will lodge. Your people shall be my people, and your God my God"* (Ruth 1:16). The two journeyed together and arrived in Bethlehem at the start of the barley harvest. The fields of Judah will become the primary setting for the remainder of the story.

Ruth committed herself to Naomi's care in a way that reflected God's loving kindness, or *hesed*. The younger widow endangered herself as a gleaner for Naomi's sake (Ruth 2:22). Gleaners collected sheaves of grain left behind on harvest fields. The Mosaic law reserved this food for *"the sojourner, the fatherless, and the widow"* (Deut. 24:19). The poor of the community needed help to survive, but compassion wasn't certain in the era of the judges. Like the Levite's concubine, a woman among strangers could be assaulted instead of protected (Ruth 2:22; Judg. 19:25). Still, Ruth set out to glean in unknown fields (Ruth 2:2). And God guided her: *"she happened to come to the part of the field belonging to Boaz, who was of the clan of Elimelech"* (Ruth 2:3).

Thanks to the narrator, the reader already knows Boaz to be a worthy man by the time Ruth's foot touches his land (Ruth 2:1). And Boaz proved his worthiness as the young widow gathered barley, and then wheat, in his field – about three months of work (Ruth 2:23).[1] Boaz displayed his own loving kindness as he charged his men not to touch Ruth. He included her in the meals provided for his laborers. He permitted her to glean – not only on the periphery of the field but among the standing sheaves. Ruth never left Boaz empty-handed (Ruth 2:8–21). He filled her arms and belly with grain. And this filled Naomi's heart with the hope of future rest.

The old widow knew God's law. Her husband and sons had died without children and Boaz was among a line of redeemers – male relatives who could serve as a proxy for the deceased by marrying his widow and producing an heir to carry his name and inheritance (Ruth 2:20; Deut. 25:5–10). This was the levirate marriage custom we saw back in Tamar's story (Gen. 38:8). Judah and his sons had neglected to perform this duty for the foreign Tamar, but the worthy Boaz might be different. Naomi directed Ruth to present the matter to him. Her suggested means of communication would replay the scene of Lot and his daughter – with an alternate ending.

Ruth washed, perfumed, and cloaked herself to visit Boaz as Naomi had commanded her (Ruth 3:1–5). The man was winnowing his grain and would remain in the field that night. After eating and drinking, Boaz went to lie down (Ruth 3:7). Ruth quietly approached the older man, one full of wine who called her a "daughter" (Ruth 2:8; 3:10). She uncovered his feet and laid down. The scenario looked too much like Lot and his daughters. The girls in that earlier story had wanted to preserve offspring for their family. Ruth was in a similar situation. Would she use seduction to achieve her means? Would Ruth and Boaz repeat the sins of their ancestors in the wilderness?

"At midnight the man was startled and turned over, and behold, a woman lay at his feet! He said, 'Who are you?' And she answered, 'I am Ruth, your servant. Spread your wings over your servant, for you are a redeemer'" (Ruth 3:8–9). Boaz awoke to find a worthy woman at his feet (Ruth 3:11). Ruth sought redemption, or a Levirate marriage, according to God's law – not sex. Boaz worked the next day to settle the matter of her redemption (Ruth 4:1–12). Boaz married Ruth and the Lord enabled conception (Ruth 4:13). Her former years of infertility ended with a son whose offspring would transition Israel from the time of the judges to a monarchy. God used a Moabite – one who did right in his eyes – to generate kings for wayward Israel and continue the line to his promised Seed. Ruth's son, Obed, would become the grandfather of King David

(Ruth 4:18–22) – and the ancestral father of Jesus the King (Mt. 1:3–6). God honors obedience above lineage.

Ruth the Moabite sits in the family tree of Christ – and with her is a family history of perverse sin. Jesus was pleased to be born into a lineage that includes Ruth. This means there's no tale of family dysfunction Jesus can't relate to. I can take it all to him in prayer. He redeemed Ruth for his glory and for our good. We see the fullness of God's *hesed* in Jesus, who came down from the Father to live as an impoverished stranger for the sake of our salvation. We can trust this King; he makes sinners members of *his* family by the redemption of his blood and enables us to live rightly in his eyes.

19

Hannah

He lifts the lowly and lowers the lofty

(1 Samuel 1 and 2:1–11)

Reflection

The God who orders everything according to his own will is pleased to use the prayers of his people to fulfill his purposes. He welcomes our bold prayers – yet he remains the Almighty sovereign who determines the outcome.

We love Cinderella-type stories for their complete plot reversals. The virtuous main character is treated cruelly by some malicious antagonist and there seems to be little hope for the suffering protagonist until a sudden (and sometimes supernatural) intervention flips the plot on its head. The despairing hero is exalted high above her former status and her tormentor is brought down by the weight of her shameful deeds. The Bible tells several stories in which the lowly is lifted and the lofty is lowered. Some of the most memorable of these are featured in 1 Samuel (David and Goliath, and David and Saul) and Hannah's account sets the tone. In her narrative, we see that *"not by might shall a man prevail"* but the sovereign Lord of Hosts determines the end (1 Sam. 2:9).

Hannah's narrative begins with the introduction of her husband, Elkanah. Like the concubine's husband in Judges 19, Elkanah was a Levite living in the hill country of Ephraim (1 Sam. 1:1). Levites were scattered among the tribes with no allotted land of their own (Josh. 21). The narrator identifies him as an "Ephraimite" because of where he lives, not his tribe. In fact, we must go to 1 Chronicles 6:16–28 to see him named a Levite. Perhaps the silence indicates what was normative of others in the period of the judges? Maybe Elkanah didn't embody the holiness required of a Levite (Lev. 21). For one, he had two wives (1 Sam. 1:2). Polygamy – a practice initiated by Cain's descendants (Gen. 4:19) – always brought unsavory results.[1] Hannah's story is an example.

Hannah is believed to be the first of Elkanah's two wives – her name is listed before Peninnah's in the narrative. Elkanah may have married Peninnah after Hannah's infertility surfaced. The text hints at Elkanah's wealth (his offering in 1 Samuel 1:24 exceeded the amount required in Numbers 15:8–10). A prominent man would be anxious for an heir. So, a day came when Hannah had to share her husband with another woman. Conception came easily for Peninnah, she gave birth to sons and daughters. Each pregnancy must have brought a sense of dishonor to Hannah's heart. And to make matters worse, Peninnah added literal insults to her injury.

Elkanah wasn't entirely neglectful of the law. He traveled yearly with his family to Shiloh, the city of God's tabernacle in those days, for appointed festivals and sacrifices (Deut. 12:1–18; 1 Sam. 1:3). The husband would give portions of the sacrificial meat to Peninnah and her children – but to Hannah, he gave a double portion (1 Sam. 1:4–5). Seeing Elkanah's favor for Hannah, Peninnah *"used to provoke her grievously to irritate her, because the Lord had closed her womb"* (1 Sam. 1:6–7). The word "irritate" here translates as "thunder against."[2] Peninnah seized this occasion for worship to blast Hannah with relentless reminders of her vacant womb

– charging God as the source. Her provocations became an annual event in the house of the Lord. And Hannah fasted and wept when she should have feasted and rejoiced (1 Sam. 1:7; Deut. 12:7).

Hannah's story is like a few we've studied thus far. In particular, she reminds us of Sarah and Rachel – favored barren wives who contended with fertile rivals (Gen. 16; 30:1–24). Hannah feels like a throwback to these Genesis matriarchs and yet her account offers something new: the benefit of her whispered prayers. She cried: "*O Lord of hosts, if you will indeed look on the affliction of your servant and remember me and not forget your servant, but will give to your servant a son, then I will give him to the Lord all the days of his life, and no razor shall touch his head*" (1 Sam. 1:11). Hannah seemed to agree with Peninnah regarding the source of her barrenness. The One who had closed her womb was also the only One who could open it.

The childless wife begged God to see her affliction, and to grant a son. She, in turn, would give the boy back to the Lord as a Nazarite. The word "Nazarite" isn't mentioned in the text, yet Hannah described one of the three conditions of the Nazarite vow. These included: avoiding wine, haircuts, and dead bodies (Num. 6:3–7). Samson, whose mother had also been barren, was made a Nazarite by God from the womb (Judg. 13:1–7). Hannah asked for a similar gift – a son separated by vow to serve the Lord.

Hannah addressed God as "the Lord of Hosts" (*Yahweh Sabaoth)* in her prayer. The name translates as "the Lord Almighty" – the one who rides before legions of armies. We might imagine this victorious title declared at the parting of the Red Sea or the conquest of Jericho, but Hannah's narrative is the first time the name appears in the Old Testament. The woman who was thundered against by a persistent adversary, needed the Lord Almighty to remember and defend her.

And the Lord Almighty remembered Hannah. He heard her prayers and, in addition to Samuel, she had three more sons and two daughters (1 Sam. 2:21). Her first child was the son of her vow, *"she called his name Samuel, for she said, 'I have asked for him from the Lord'"* (1 Sam. 1:20). Samuel grew to be Israel's last and greatest judge. He anointed the nation's first two kings – Saul and David (1 Sam. 10:1; 16:13). God remembered Hannah and granted her the very son who would shepherd Israel from a judiciary to a monarchy – a change Hannah herself seemed to anticipate (1 Sam. 2:10). God worked through her prayer to establish his will for her and for his covenant people. The Almighty sovereign who orders all things according to the counsel of his own will, was pleased to use the quiet prayers of a barren woman to fulfill his purposes (Eph. 1:11).

Hannah's narrative concludes with a poetic prayer in Chapter 2. Her struggle with infertility had been a battle. So, like a singing Miriam and Deborah before their defeated foe, she exalted the General of Heaven in song (Ex. 15:1–21; Judg. 5; 1 Sam. 2:1–10). The Lord of Hosts had lifted the humble Hannah but thundered against her boastful rival (1 Sam. 2:8–10). Her story ended with a God-wrought reversal. Mary, the mother of Christ, takes up Hannah's tune in her Magnificat (Lk. 1:46–55). Mary magnifies the God who raises the lowly but scatters the proud. Her Son would embody her and Hannah's hymns as the humble Christ – persecuted and killed by arrogant men but raised and enthroned as the King of Kings (1 Sam. 2:8; Lk. 1:52). The gospel is a story of a God-wrought reversal. Those who lower themselves in repentance are lifted up in Mary's exalted Son. That Son fights our battles. Power and mercy are his – we can trust our prayers and stories to Christ, the Almighty One.

And the women who lived in the days of Israel's monarchy will look to this higher king in Part Five of the book.

PART FIVE:

Women from Israel's Monarchy to the Exile

20

Abigail

The mediator who turns away wrath

(1 Samuel 25)

Reflection

God has provided for us a Mediator to appease the wrath incurred by our sins. The wise woman will look to this Savior and not her own vain salvation.

The opening scene of Abigail's story features Samuel's death. *"Now Samuel died. And all Israel assembled and mourned for him, and they buried him in his house at Ramah"* (1 Sam. 25:1). Hannah's son had been a faithful judge. He appointed his two sons as judges after him while still alive. But his sons were wicked – and Israel dismissed them. The people demanded a king instead. They wanted an earthly monarch like other nations (1 Sam. 8:5). The request displeased Samuel but God replied with these words: *"they have not rejected you, but they have rejected me from being king over them. According to all the deeds that they have done, from the day I brought them up out of Egypt even to this day, forsaking me and serving other gods, so they are also doing to you"* (1 Sam. 8:7–9). With this, Samuel anointed Saul, then David (1 Sam. 10; 16). At last, Israel had the royal rulers anticipated in the book of Judges. Yet, we see here that the nation had always had a Sovereign – she simply chose self-autonomy according to her own wisdom (Judg. 21:25). Interestingly, Abigail's account will be a contrast between the wise who look to God and the foolish who glory in their own ways.

Abigail was the wife of a wealthy man named Nabal. Her husband was rich in livestock but lacking in character. He's described as *"harsh and badly behaved"* (1 Sam. 25:3). He was a Calebite, or a descendant of Caleb (1 Sam. 25:2–3). You'll remember Caleb as one of the twelve spies sent by Moses to survey the Promised Land (Num. 13 – 14). Caleb and Joshua brought a faithful report to the people and, for this reason, they were the only two of Moses' generation to enter Canaan (Josh. 14:6–15). Caleb was given Hebron, a city in the territory of Judah (Josh. 15:13), about eight miles from Nabal's hometown of Maon.[1] Apparently Nabal inherited his ancestor's land – but not his faith. This deficiency would ultimately lead his wife Abigail to face the wrath of four hundred warriors.

It happened that Nabal's shepherds were in the wilderness of Paran at the same time as David. He had been anointed by Samuel to replace a disobedient King Saul (1 Sam. 13:13–14). Unfortunately for David, Saul remained enthroned, envious, and at his heels. David – with a band of six hundred fighting men – was likely evading Saul in Paran. His men assumed the duty of protecting Nabal's herdsmen while there. They served as a "wall" around these workers, shielding them day and night from danger (1 Sam. 25:4–7, 14–16). They maintained this position until the day of shearing – a festive day of rejoicing over the abundance of sheared wool. The Mosaic law called for hospitality and generosity at harvest and feast times (Deut. 24:19–22). Knowing this, David sent messengers to greet Nabal. He hoped to receive whatever the older man was willing to offer in recognition of his service and for the sustenance of his men (1 Sam. 25:6–8). Unfortunately, Nabal chose to humiliate David instead of demonstrating grateful hospitality.

Perhaps Abigail was away when David's greeting arrived. She missed his men for some reason (1 Sam. 25:25). The messengers were left to Nabal's company, and he railed sarcastically at them: *"Who is David? Who is the son of Jesse? There are many servants these days who are breaking away from their masters. Shall I take my bread and my water and my meat that I have killed for my shearers and give it to men who come from I do not know where?"* (1 Sam. 25:10–11). The repetition of "my" four times in Nabal's address highlights the man's self-centeredness. In his rude response he sought to disrespect David further by pretending he had no knowledge of him. This, however, was unlikely.

David was the great slayer of Goliath (1 Sam. 17:50–51). All Israel sang of his victories (1 Sam. 18:6–7). He was presently a wanderer wanted by King Saul, nevertheless *Yahweh* had anointed him king. Abigail would later affirm this (1 Sam. 25:30–31) – so why didn't Nabal? Especially when the Judean David had been anointed in the region of the Calebites. Apparently, this wasn't a matter of Nabal's ignorance but rather his indifference to God's promise through Samuel. The man knew David's story but chose to highlight his status as a disfavored fugitive servant of Saul. He repaid David's good deed with evil by emphasizing his lowered position. This was a sign of Nabal's disregard of *Yahweh* himself.

The foolish man's untamed tongue fueled the flames of David's anger and a fire threatened to consume Nabal (1 Sam. 25:34; Jas. 3:5–6). David had sheltered his men in the desert, now he would slaughter Nabal's men. He said to his troops, *"'Every man strap on his sword!' And every man of them strapped on his sword. David also strapped on his sword. And about four hundred men went up after David"* (1 Sam. 25:13). David vowed to murder Nabal and his family (1 Sam. 25:22). And here, Abigail steps onto the stage of the narrative.

The woman enters the scene like a busy triage nurse, assessing damage and treating wounds. It's immediately clear that the safety of Nabal's household rested on Abigail's wisdom. A servant came to inform her of the impending disaster and looked to her for their salvation (1 Sam. 25:14–17). Abigail made haste and gathered large portions of food and drink – displaying generosity where Nabal had shown greediness. She laid these provisions on donkeys and set out to meet David (1 Sam. 25:18–20). One unarmed woman heading toward four hundred swordsmen.

We are not given Abigail's thoughts as she rode to face a vengeful David. Was she nervous? Was this the first time she was working to rescue Nabal, or one of countless occasions? Did she feel anger toward his imprudence? Did she replay the events that had made her the wife of a worthless man? We have no answers, but this we might venture: Abigail's thoughts were perhaps on God's Word as she rode, for this would be her defense before David.

The woman saw the warriors and prostrated herself on the ground before David, their leader. She said: *"On me alone, my lord, be the guilt … Please forgive the trespass of your servant. For the LORD will certainly make my lord a sure house, because my lord is fighting the battles of the LORD, and evil shall not be found in you so long as you live"* (1 Sam. 25:24–28). Abigail's speech ought to impress us. She was willing to bear Nabal's guilt and take the punishment due her unworthy husband to save the lives of the males in her household. She gives us the picture of a wise mediator, full of truth. Abigail recalled God's promises to David while reminding him that vengeance belonged to *Yahweh*: *"And when the LORD has done to my lord according to all the good that he has spoken concerning you and has appointed you prince over Israel, my lord shall have no cause of grief or pangs of conscience for having shed blood without cause or for my lord working salvation himself"* (1 Sam. 25:30–31). This woman met the force of four hundred warriors with soft answers that turned away wrath (Prov. 15:1). Her words became the means of salvation for her household, and a means of grace to David.

David's heart went from rage to worship. He exclaimed: *"Blessed be the LORD, the God of Israel, who sent you this day to meet me! Blessed be your discretion, and blessed be you, who have kept me this day from bloodguilt and from working salvation with my own hand!"* (1 Sam. 25:32–33). Abigail's mediation had kept David from reacting as foolishly as the self-centered Nabal. David turned back to the wilderness and left vengeance to *Yahweh*. The Judge of Israel rode onward to Nabal and struck him to death ten days after this incident (1 Sam. 25:38). Abigail was widowed – but not for long. David requested her hand and she rode to him again – this time as his wife (1 Sam. 25:39–42). Abigail is chronicled as the second wife of David, the king of Israel (1 Chr. 3:1).

Abigail was a masterful communicator, her persuasive ability to reach the heart of a vengeful David was brilliant. But in Abigail, we see something even more stunning: a foreshadow of Christ, the wise mediator (1 Tim 2:5). Our self-centered hearts disregard God's authority in many ways. We are sinners who have earned his righteous anger. Our hope for pardon rests in Christ alone, a mediator even better than Abigail. He charged forward to face God's just wrath on our behalf and offered not just wisdom but his own life. Jesus bore the guilt of our sinful folly and conquered the death owed for our transgressions (2 Cor. 5:21). Friend, let your heart fear the Lord – for to do so is the beginning of wisdom (Prov. 1:7). But the fool regards their own wisdom and authority.

21

Bathsheba

A washing of the soul God alone oversees

(2 Samuel 11 – 12)

Reflection

You can't escape the curse of eternal death by making yourself clean before God. Jesus, Bathsheba's ancestral Son, died to take on the death of his people.

It seems that death is a transitional marker in the story of the Bible. If you flip to the start of Parts Two through Five of this book, you will find death ushering the narrative along. These sections feature obituaries that remind us of our need for God's promised Seed – one able to deliver us from death (Gen. 3:15). We begin with Saul's passing in this chapter.

The book of 1 Samuel concludes with Saul's demise. His death didn't trigger the national mourning we saw at Samuel's burial (1 Sam. 25:1) and Scripture narrows its focus to the grieving of a single individual: David. The number one person on Saul's hit list was presumably the loudest mourner at his passing. Second Samuel opens with David lamenting Saul and his son Jonathan (2 Sam. 1:17–27). The book then transitions to a civil war that establishes David's kingship over all Israel (2 Sam. 5:1–5). Next, *Yahweh* visits King David through the prophet Nathan and makes a covenant with him. God said to David in 2 Samuel 7:9–13:

> *I will make for you a great name, like the name of the great ones of the earth. And I will appoint a place for my people Israel and will plant them, so that they may dwell in their own place and be disturbed no more... Moreover, the LORD declares to you that the LORD will make you a house. When your days are fulfilled and you lie down with your fathers, I will raise up your offspring after you, who shall come from your body, and I will establish his kingdom. He shall build a house for my name, and I will establish the throne of his kingdom forever.*

We call these verses the Davidic Covenant and they are as significant as the Abrahamic Covenant (Gen. 12:1–3, 7). In fact, the guarantees made to Abraham of a great name, place, and offspring come to rest on David.[1] The former fugitive becomes the royal recipient of promises that pointed back to Abraham and looked forward to a promised Seed. David's kingdom appears firm and full of righteousness – until 2 Samuel 11. There, God's elected king despises God's Word.

In the spring – the time when kings went out to battle – David sent his military commander and troops to war but he remains at his house in Jerusalem. The king spends a lazy afternoon relaxing on the roof of his palace. Homes in ancient Israel were built with side stairs leading up to a flat roof. These spaces provided a cool area for storage or sleeping, as seen in Rahab's account (Josh. 2:6).

David's elevated roof afforded a view of the homes below and his attention was drawn to a particular scene – a woman bathing (2 Sam. 11:1–2). The narrator will later explain that this was not a bath of luxury but of ceremony.

The Mosaic law declared a woman unclean for seven days during her menstrual cycle. Afterwards, she was to cleanse herself by washing (Lev. 15:19–28). Scripture tells us that the bathing woman, Bathsheba, *"had been purifying herself from her uncleanness"* (2 Sam. 11:4). Perhaps the same spring weather that sent David to the roof also led Bathsheba to conduct her ritual cleansing in some airy corner of her courtyard. We can only speculate since the passage doesn't specify her exact location. But we do know this: the king of Israel stood atop watching a ceremony intended for the Lord alone.

David inquired about the woman, and she was identified as *"Bathsheba, the daughter of Eliam, the wife of Uriah the Hittite"* (2 Sam. 11:3). The narrator paints the next scene with quick verbs that avoid graphic details yet convey a clear picture: *"So David sent messengers and took her, and she came to him, and he lay with her"* (2 Sam. 11:4). Weeks later, Bathsheba sent a three-word message: *"I am pregnant"* (2 Sam. 11:5). Each day her period was late must have brought Bathsheba more anxiety. Yet the narrator doesn't share her personal thoughts. Apart from her short note, the woman doesn't speak in this narrative. Her silence recalls that of the Levite's concubine, a woman brutally assaulted in Judges 19 without a word. Although Bathsheba came from a family accustomed to public attention, she maintained her privacy through her silence.

The pregnant Bathsheba came from a politically connected family. This might in fact explain her proximity to the king's palace. Her father was Eliam, one of King David's thirty mighty men (2 Sam. 11:3; 23:8–39). Ahithophel of Gilo was Eliam's father and Bathsheba's grandfather.[2] Ahithophel was also one of David's trusted counselors (2 Sam. 15:12). His later involvement in this drama will thicken an already dense plot. Ahithophel will direct Absalom, David's mutinous son, to sleep openly with his father's ten concubines on the palace roof – the very location of David's voyeurism (2 Sam. 16:20–23). Perhaps Ahithophel's guidance was the revenge of a bitter grandfather. Whatever the case, Absalom's act became poetic justice against David's evil deeds, which included sexual violation and murder (2 Sam. 12:11–12).

Bathsheba's husband, Uriah the Hittite, is also mentioned among David's mighty men (2 Sam. 23:39). The loyal Uriah was a foreigner with a Hebrew name meaning "the LORD is my light."[3] The faithful soldier sacrificed marital enjoyments for the sake of *Yahweh* and his people, while David stole these pleasures for himself (2 Sam. 11:11). David, who had avoided bloodguilt in Abigail's account, plotted the murder of Uriah to cover up Bathsheba's pregnancy (1 Sam. 25:33; 2 Sam. 11:6–17). The news of Uriah's death reached Bathsheba: "*When the wife of Uriah heard that Uriah her husband was dead, she lamented over her husband. And when the mourning was over, David sent and brought her to his house, and she became his wife and bore him a son*" (2 Sam. 11:26–27).

We're not given the details of Bathsheba's lamentations. We're left to wonder how she managed the stages of grief and transition from Uriah's only wife to one of David's many (1 Chr. 3:1–9). Bathsheba maintained her silence – but *Yahweh* spoke.

God sends Nathan back to the king (2 Sam. 12:1) – but, this time, it is not to affirm covenant blessings. The prophet pronounces a curse, because "*the thing that David had done displeased the LORD*" (2 Sam. 11:27). Nathan tells a parable, recounting David's wicked actions. His crimes were like that of a rich man who seized, slaughtered, and ate the only pet lamb of his poor neighbor (2 Sam. 12:1–6). David had cruelly robbed Uriah and consumed Bathsheba like mere meat. He tossed aside at least three of God's Ten Commandments: he coveted his neighbor's wife, he committed adultery, and he committed murder (Ex. 20:17, 14, 13). King David had scorned God and his Word. Because of this, violence and evil would fester in his home (2 Sam. 12:11–12) and the infant son born to him would die (2 Sam. 12:14). According to the Mosaic law, David himself was worthy of death (Lev. 20:10; 24:17).

Yet we hear this from Nathan: "*The LORD also has put away your sin; you shall not die*" (2 Sam. 12:13).

Why? After all, God doesn't hide our sins under a rug or in some dark filing cabinet – he deals with sin.

So why does David live?

David admitted his sin (2 Sam. 12:13). Elsewhere in Scripture, he cries: *"Wash me thoroughly from my iniquity, and cleanse me from my sin!"* (Ps. 51:2). This was a washing of the soul *Yahweh* alone would oversee. God heard the repentant David and put his sin onto Another. David's sin would fall on the head of his greater Son by covenant promise. Jesus is the Son who ultimately dies in his place, taking on the punishment demanded by the law. And who is listed as an ancestral mother of this great Son? It's not wise Abigail, or another of David's many wives, but Bathsheba (Mt. 1:6). In mercy, Bathsheba continues the line that ends with King Jesus. The shed blood of Bathsheba's distant Son cleanses everyone who admits their sins to him – no matter how filthy those sins may be (1 Jn. 1:7).

22

Tamar

He gives them beauty for ashes

(2 Samuel 13)

Reflection

Christ willingly entered the world of sin and suffered shame and injustice at the hand of sinners. He can sympathize with Tamar's cry.

We have the stories of two women named Tamar in Scripture. We met the first one back in Genesis 38. The Tamar of Genesis 38, a neglected widow, disguised herself as a prostitute and slept with Judah, her father-in-law, to conceive an heir for her provision and the perpetuation of her husband's line. She conceived twin sons and one of them, Perez, continued the covenant line that led to King David (Ruth 4:18–22).

David became the father of the Bible's second Tamar. The story of Tamar number two is told in 2 Samuel 13. Her story involves sex as well – but not like the first. David's eldest son Amnon rapes Tamar, his half-sister. And the incident harkens back to the sins of ancestors long gone.

David had several sons from his many wives (1 Chr. 3:1–9). The first-born was Amnon, and Absalom was the third by a different mother. Our passage identifies Tamar as Absalom's beautiful sister (2 Sam. 13:2). Now Scripture doesn't often name a daughter unless the woman is involved in a narrative. We see this with Jacob's daughter Dinah (Gen. 30:21). Genesis 37:35 mentions Jacob's "sons and daughters" but Dinah, whose rape is described in Genesis 34, is the only daughter specified. The inclusion of Tamar's name in 2 Samuel 13 is a hint to us that she will be a central figure in the narrative. And the narrator doesn't waste any time in telling that tale. Verse 1 concludes like this: *"And after a time Amnon, David's son, loved her."* Amnon's love for Tamar wasn't the familial affection of a sibling – it was the lustful obsession of a man desperate to ravish a woman, in this case, his own half-sister.

"And Amnon was so tormented that he made himself ill because of his sister Tamar, for she was a virgin, and it seemed impossible to Amnon to do anything to her" (2 Sam. 13:2). As the virgin daughter of the king, Tamar was sexually inaccessible to men.[1] A beautiful virgin daughter was an asset to a monarch. In the ancient Near Eastern world of political bargaining, a princess who remained a virgin might enter the palace of another king as the prize of an alliance. Tamar's mother, Maacah, was herself the daughter of Talmai, King of Geshur (1 Chr. 3:2). David had married a foreign princess – and royalty on both sides of Tamar's DNA positioned her as a potential future queen in some court. Likely, her expectation and hope was to remain a virgin and marry well. As a presumably pampered prince, Amnon was unaccustomed to restraint and pouted over this situation until it made him sick.

Here, our narrator introduces a new character who acts and sounds a lot like the ancient serpent at the Fall. *"Amnon had a friend, whose name was Jonadab, the son of Shimeah, David's brother. And Jonadab was a very crafty man"* (2 Sam. 13:3). Jonadab was a cousin, counselor, and companion to Amnon. He is called "crafty" – the very word used to describe the serpent in Genesis 3:1. And just like the probing snake, Jonadab enters the narrative with interrogations. He asks Amnon: "*'O son of the king, why are you so haggard morning after morning? Will you not tell me?' Amnon said to him, 'I love Tamar, my brother Absalom's sister'*" (2 Sam. 13:4). The name Tamar means "Palm Tree."[2] Because they were related, sex with her was as forbidden to Amnon as that one tree had been to Adam and Eve (Gen. 2:17; Deut. 27:22). Just as Eve was misguided by the snake's subtle persuasion, Amnon was encouraged to sin because of Jonadab's cunning counsel. His cousin directed him to feign some illness that would send King David coming to check on him. Once there, he could request bread baked and served fresh by the hand of Tamar. Amnon played the part written by Jonadab and David sent Tamar into her half-brother's house (2 Sam. 13:5–8). The young lady would never be the same after this visit.

Tamar took dough, kneaded it, and baked cakes while Amnon lay watching (2 Sam. 13:8). His lewd voyeurism flashes to David's spectator view of Bathsheba, as he stood atop his roof observing the woman bathe. The narrative will trigger more scenes from the past as we will see. Tamar served the bread to her brother, but he refused to eat. The crown prince ordered everyone to leave the room but Tamar (2 Sam. 13:9–10). He then took hold of her and demanded sex. "*Come, lie with me, my sister*" were his words (2 Sam. 13:11).

I worked a part-time job as an intake counselor at a domestic violence shelter for women while in seminary. Some of the women we served arrived at our safe home with purple and blue bruises on their faces and bodies. The stories they told of abuse by men in their homes were awful, to say the least. I can't help but think of these women as I read Tamar's desperate pleas to prevent her half-brother's abuse.

She answers him in verses 12–13:

> *No, my brother, do not violate me, for such a thing is not done in Israel; do not do this outrageous thing. As for me, where could I carry my shame? And as for you, you would be as one of the outrageous fools in Israel. Now therefore, please speak to the king, for he will not withhold me from you.*

In the account of David and Bathsheba, we have silence. Not so with Tamar. The girl didn't have the physical strength to fight her brother, but she charged at him with the force of wisdom. She reminded Amnon of the outrageousness of rape and incest among God's people (Deut. 22:23–24; 27:22). She pointed to the emotional damage such an assault would cause her and the destruction to his own reputation. She concluded her appeal with a suggestion: seek marriage as the route to sex. We don't know if David would have indeed sanctioned the union of these siblings, but Tamar was determined to overcome her opponent with reason. Abigail had crushed David's murderous passion with wise words (1 Sam. 25:33). But Amnon walked in the way of Nabal. He wouldn't listen to Tamar – and being stronger than she was, he raped her (2 Sam. 13:14).

According to the Mosaic law, a man who assaulted a virgin was compelled to marry her without divorce (Deut. 22:28–29). This guaranteed care for the woman whose hopes for another marriage would have been dashed. Shechem, Dinah's rapist, had desired marriage after his assault (Gen. 34:8–12). Amnon, on the other hand, dragged Tamar out of his home. His supposed "love" for her morphed into hatred once she became a victim of his perversion (2 Sam. 13:15). Tamar left knowing that she would likely never wed. *"And Tamar put ashes on her head and tore the long robe that she wore. And she laid her hand on her head and went away, crying aloud as she went"* (2 Sam. 13:19). Given her current circumstances, her only expectation was to live in the house of her brother Absalom under his care. Absalom, like the sons of Jacob, would soon kill Amnon for molesting his sister (2 Sam. 13:28–29; Gen. 34:26–27). We observe that David sat passively as this family drama unfolds (2 Sam. 13:20–22).

There are moments in Scripture where we see an immediate escalation of sin from parent to child. Adam and Eve and their son Cain is the first occasion of this: the parents who stole fruit were followed by a son who robbed them of another child, the fruit of their womb (Gen. 3:6; 4:8). The murder of Cain would be the first of many acts of domestic violence among Adam's progenies. The rape of Tamar reveals another instance of heightened sin between a parent and child – this time between David and Amnon. David's transgression against his neighbor's wife came to roost under his own roof as his daughter is molested by his firstborn son. Perhaps news of the rape brought back *Yahweh*'s words from the prophet Nathan: *"Behold, I will raise up evil against you out of your own house"* (2 Sam. 12:11). David abandoned his sons to their sins and his assaulted daughter to her lonely desolation. Did the shameful memory of his own crime hinder his fatherly discipline and his kingly justice?

My job as an intake counselor at a domestic violence shelter offered some opportunity to tell battered women about a greater Father. This One didn't rule with passivity but sent his only Son to address evil in the world. Jesus, God's Son – like us in every respect but for our sin (Heb. 2:17; 4:15) – knows firsthand what it's like to be afflicted and abused by wicked people. He can sympathize with Tamar's cry. He suffered the injustice of a Roman cross, despising the shame. But Jesus conquered evil on that cross and is seated today *"at the right hand of the throne of God"* (Heb. 12:2). He welcomes women like Tamar into his royal court, not on the condition of their virginity, but based on the pure righteousness he himself suffered to give them. He is the King anointed *"to proclaim the year of the LORD's favor, and the day of vengeance of our God; to comfort all who mourn ... to give them a beautiful headdress instead of ashes"* (Is. 61:1–3; Lk. 4:16–19). No desolate woman is without hope in his kingdom.

23

Rizpah

A sinless King on a higher throne

(2 Samuel 21)

Reflection

Earthly sovereigns will ultimately take more than they give. But there is a King on a higher throne who gives himself to bring us peace with God.

Of the thirty biblical women featured in this book, Rizpah is likely to be the least well known. Almost every person I spoke with while writing it had never heard of her. Rizpah was Saul's concubine and she is mentioned within a larger drama involving powerful kings, a broken oath, famine, execution by hanging, and propitiatory justice. In short, the plotline is intense. The story is found near the end of the book of 2 Samuel and it's darker than any fictional folklore that the Grimm brothers could have produced. Rizpah held a lengthy vigil over the dead bodies of her sons and her actions moved the mercy of the king of Israel – and the King of Heaven.

At some point during David's forty-year kingship, Israel suffered a three-year famine (2 Sam. 21:1; 5:4). David sought the Lord on the cause and was told, *"There is bloodguilt on Saul and on his house, because he put the Gibeonites to death"* (2 Sam. 21:1). You might remember that David himself had bloodguilt on his hands in the matter of Uriah the Hittite and God's judgment had landed squarely on his household. It seems that Saul had committed a similar sin – although in his case, the entire nation was suffering the consequences. The reason for the distinction was tied to the identity of their respective victims. David violated his neighbor's house and therefore evil visited his own (2 Sam. 12:9–11). Saul broke a fateful national oath by slaughtering the people of Gibeon, and therefore a famine overtook all Israel.

Israel and Gibeon had a long history beginning back in Joshua 9. Joshua and a young Israel had just conquered the cities of Jericho and Ai. They were encouraged to press onward in their conquest of the Promised Land when a delegation of raggedly attired tribesmen approached seeking a peace treaty. The group claimed to be travelers from a distant country, thus their worn-out appearance. They had heard of *Yahweh's* victories in Egypt and in the desert and had journeyed to establish friendship. Now Israel was to put the Canaanites to the sword – not make covenants with them (Deut. 7:1–2). Joshua should have sought the wisdom of God before acting, but he didn't. He and the people were easily swayed based on the appearance of the supposed travelers and vowed peace to them in the name of the Lord. Three days later, Joshua learned that the men were Gibeonites living among them in Canaan (Josh. 9:1–27). They had deceived Israel.

Joshua made the Gibeonites cutters of wood and drawers of water for the altar of the Lord (Josh. 9:27). The people of Gibeon would dwell among Israel as servants, but Joshua warned: *"let them live, lest wrath be upon us, because of the oath that we swore to them"* (Josh. 9:20). But Saul had ignored this caution and had slaughtered many of the Gibeonites.

Now, the wrath that Joshua had feared had come in the form of a relentless drought and David faced a crisis created by his dead predecessor. In an attempt to make things right with the Gibeonites, he asked them: *"What shall I do for you? And how shall I make atonement, that you may bless the heritage of the LORD"* (2 Sam. 21:3). The Gibeonites didn't want money or a chance to massacre Israel. They wanted full expiation, an act of atonement, and demanded that seven of Saul's sons die before the Lord as payment (seven was the number of completion) (2 Sam. 21:4–6). King David agreed to their request without hesitation. Seven men from Saul's linage were sentenced to death with few words: "I will give them" (2 Sam. 21:6).Two of these men would be the sons of Rizpah and Saul.

"The king took the two sons of Rizpah the daughter of Aiah, whom she bore to Saul, Armoni and Mephibosheth" (2 Sam. 21:8).[1] Furthermore, *"the five sons of Merab the daughter of Saul, whom she bore to Adriel the son of Barzillai the Meholathite"* – in other words, five of Saul's grandsons would also be hung by the Gibeonites. The news must have sent shockwaves through the mothers of these men. Here we also notice God's oracle of pain in motherhood isn't limited to infertility and labor contractions – sadly, it can include the death of a child (Gen. 3:16). I know women who have buried children and they say few sorrows can compare. Rizpah would soon know this anguish.

Rizpah's life had been a perilous one long before her sons were drafted to die for the sins of their father. As a concubine in the court of cunning men she had long been a pawn in a game of political chess. After the death of Saul, Israel's allegiance was divided between two men – David and Saul's son, Ish-bosheth (2 Sam. 2). Ish-bosheth ruled as a figurehead with true power resting in the hands of Abner, the commander of Saul's army. At some point, Ish-bosheth accused Abner of sleeping with Rizpah (2 Sam. 3:6–9). The narrator neither denies nor affirms the charge but this accusation was serious, to say the least! To sleep with a king's wife or concubine was to make a direct claim for the throne – hence Absalom slept with David's concubines in his insurrection (2 Sam. 16:20–22). In this case, Rizpah was a point of contention in a chaotic fight for power that would end with the death of both Abner and Ish-bosheth (2 Sam. 3 – 5). And now her connection to Israel's throne would once again result in death – this time, the death of her two precious sons.

David turned the seven sons of Saul over to the Gibeonites, and *"they hanged them on the mountain before the LORD, and the seven of them perished together. They were put to death in the first days of harvest, at the beginning of barley harvest"* (2 Sam. 21:9). Now, according to Mosaic law, a person hanged was cursed by God and was to be buried on the same day of their death (Deut. 21:22–23). An exposed body would defile the land. King David was attempting to right a wrong for the restoration of the land and yet he ignored this commandment for some reason and didn't take the men's bodies down. It's at this point that the narrator shines a spotlight on Rizpah in a stirring yet melancholic role.

The bereaved mother took sackcloth for herself and spread it on a rock near the lifeless bodies of her children. She would remain in this position *"from the beginning of harvest until rain fell upon them from the heavens. And she did not allow the birds of the air to come upon them by day, or the beasts of the field by night"* (2 Sam. 21:10). We can't say how long Rizpah maintained her ominous watch. Reapers in ancient Israel harvested the barley crop in late April and looked for heavy rains in October.[2] A six-month vigil seems unreasonably long so perhaps Rizpah intended to remain in her position until *Yahweh* responded to the expiatory death of her sons with rain?

Her act was daring, whatever its length. This woman, accustomed to court luxuries, left every known comfort. She shrouded a rock in sackcloth, the sign of mourning, and made it her home. Day and night she suffered the putrid stench of seven decaying men. She fought plundering birds by day, and by night she stood sleeplessly over the bodies of her family so that they might not suffer the final disgrace of becoming carrion for scavenging beasts (Deut. 28:26). With the resolve of a self-sacrificing mother, Rizpah wouldn't leave until her sons were put to rest.

David was struck by the news of Rizpah's determination. He proceeded – whether by shame or inspiration – to bury the men as required by the law. And not only that, but he also took the bones of Saul and Jonathan and buried them with the seven killed by the Gibeonites in the tomb of Kish, their forefather. *Yahweh's* wrath was appeased only at the completed work of the king, and he responded to the plea for the land (2 Sam. 21:11–14).

Rizpah's story appears to be tucked away in a lesser-known corner of the Old Testament, but it begs attention. Her sons died to satisfy a debt owed by another, King Saul. A monarch was supposed to bring justice and righteousness, not the propitiatory death of his children. Rizpah's grief for her boys resounds God's warning to Israel: your sons and daughters will suffer on account of your kings (1 Sam. 8:10–18). The swaying bodies of her sons encircled by vultures were the result of a broken oath made by an earthly king. But there is a much better King, who faithfully keeps his word and whose court is free from sin. King Jesus laid down his own life and was hung on a tree for the atonement of sin. He became a curse and died, not just for one man, but for all who trust in him (1 Jn. 2:2; Rom. 3:21–26). And unlike the sons of Rizpah, this King rose from the grave to greet the women who kept vigil at his death (Jn. 20:11–18). He is now preparing a place where there is no darkness, death, or despair (Rev. 21:4). My friend, look not to the "kings" of your own making but to the sinless King on a higher throne.

24

The Widow of Zarephath

God provides for an unexpected provider

(1 Kings 17)

Reflection

God's kingdom comprises all the families of the earth – people redeemed not by their merit or genealogy, but by faith in the death and resurrection of the life-giving Son.

The account of the Widow of Zarephath comes several centuries after the Davidic Kingdom. We saw earlier that life under David's rule had been far from perfect. Bathsheba, Tamar, and Rizpah could affirm that. David was deeply flawed – yet which of us are accepted by God according to our merit? Rather, *"Blessed is the one whose transgression is forgiven ... against whom the LORD counts no iniquity, and in whose spirit there is no deceit"* (Ps. 32:1–2). David didn't succumb to the pretense of hiding his sins – he confessed all and was forgiven all. King David's devotion to *Yahweh* would become the standard by which every Judean king would be measured. Some would meet the mark, but many would fall short, beginning with his successor Solomon.

"Now King Solomon loved many foreign women ... from the nations concerning which the Lord *had said to the people of Israel, 'You shall not enter into marriage with them ... for surely they will turn away your heart after their gods.' Solomon clung to these in love"* (1 Kgs. 11:1–2). Solomon chose the embrace of his forbidden wives over the law of God. For this, *Yahweh* ripped the kingdom from the hands of his heir, Rehoboam (1 Kgs. 12:1–24). Still, the Lord remembered his covenant with David and for the sake of his faithfulness, he reserved two tribes for the house of David – Judah and Benjamin in the south (1 Kgs. 11:9–13). The remaining ten northern tribes went to a man named Jeroboam. King Jeroboam was quick to build the northern kingdom on a foundation of idolatry (1 Kgs. 12:25–33). This sin would endure long after him, with every successive northern king becoming increasingly unfaithful to God. Wicked Ahab is a case in point. He was the sixth king after Jeroboam and he *"did evil in the sight of the* Lord*, more than all who were before him"* (1 Kgs. 16:30).

Each king in the period of Israel's monarchy seemed to have a prophet divinely assigned to him with the ministry of exhorting, rebuking, and warning according to the Word of the Lord. David had Nathan; Ahab had Elijah the Tishbite. We meet this fiery prophet in 1 Kings 17, and his first words to Ahab announce judgment: *"As the* Lord*, the God of Israel, lives, before whom I stand, there shall be neither dew nor rain these years, except by my word"* (1 Kgs. 17:1). Drought, one of the many curses for covenant unfaithfulness, was coming to Israel (Deut. 28:22–24). With this pronouncement, both Elijah and the rain left the scene for three and a half long years. God would send his prophet to strange places, including the Sidonian city of Zarephath.

When God uses you to bring famine to your lawless nation, you instantly become a fugitive. Outlawed, Elijah fled to a brook named Cherith, east of the Jordan River, to hide.[1] He found water there and the Lord instructed ravens to feed him bread and meat twice daily

(1 Kgs. 17:3–6). This continued until the brook dried, and God redirected Elijah: *"Arise, go to Zarephath, which belongs to Sidon, and dwell there. Behold, I have commanded a widow there to feed you"* (1 Kgs. 17:9). *Yahweh* was using a widow to deliver his prophet from starvation. The thought of this is astounding when we consider the story of Ruth. Widows were generally among the poorest in the society, especially in times of famine, which is why the Mosaic law provided terms for their care (Lev. 23:22; Deut. 24:19–21). How then could this lone woman sustain herself in addition to looking after a grown man? My instinct would have been to question God, but Elijah's was immediate obedience: *"So he arose and went to Zarephath"* (1 Kgs. 17:10).

As his feet touched the gates of Zarephath, the prophet looked up to find a widow collecting sticks. He recognized her as God's means of provision for him and requested water and a small piece of bread. Her response wasn't promising:

> *As the Lord your God lives, I have nothing baked, only a handful of flour in a jar and a little oil in a jug. And now I am gathering a couple of sticks that I may go in and prepare it for myself and my son, that we may eat it and die"* (1 Kgs. 17:12).

The single mother was down to her last bit of food. She had been planning a final meal for herself and her son when Elijah interrupted with a demand for bread. Her reply referred to the Lord by his covenant name, but she makes it clear that he was Elijah's God – not hers. This Sidonian was not a servant of *Yahweh*. The ravens had obeyed God's directive to serve Elijah. Would this widow trust his Word enough to obey?

The woman must have hesitated. After all, giving your child's last meal to a visitor during a famine would be difficult for any mother – even one living in a culture of hospitality. Perhaps her struggle was visible, for the prophet offered words of comfort. He said to her:

> *Do not fear; go and do as you have said. But first make me a little cake of it and bring it to me, and afterward make something for yourself and your son. For thus says the* Lord, *the God of Israel, "The jar of flour shall not be spent, and the jug of oil shall not be empty, until the day that the* Lord *sends rain upon the earth" (1 Kgs. 17:13–14).*

The prophet's assurance prevailed over the widow's anxieties – at least enough for her to extend the welcome of an ancient Near Eastern host. The widow offered her scanty fare to Elijah and was met with steady provision for her own household. Unlike the brook Cherith, her jar of flour and jug of oil flowed until the rains came (1 Kgs. 17:16). We might expect the narrative to end after this happy resolution to Elijah and the widow. However, the threat of death still loomed even though they had bread to eat.

"After this the son of the woman, the mistress of the house, became ill. And his illness was so severe that there was no breath left in him" (1 Kgs. 17:17). The widow's son died. His mother had anticipated his, and her own, death before meeting Elijah. But why should her son die now that the Lord was sustaining them with food? Perhaps this question had plagued the bereaved mother, for she approached Elijah with an impassioned remark: *"What have you against me, O man of God? You have come to me to bring my sin to remembrance and to cause the death of my son"* (1 Kgs. 17:18)! She blamed the prophet for her loss. From her perspective, he had come to reveal her sins and the prophet's God had taken her son as payment. Elijah didn't meet this charge with a defense. He simply took the boy's body from her and went to petition God (1 Kgs. 17:19–21). The widow had opened her pantry to *Yahweh*'s servant to find her empty vessels replenished. Now her lifeless boy was in Elijah's arms, would her son also revive?

Elijah prayed and the Lord listened to him, *"the life of the child came into him again, and he revived"* (1 Kgs. 17:22). The prophet returned the child to his mother, and she received him with new faith. She said to

Elijah: *"Now I know that you are a man of God, and that the word of the* LORD *in your mouth is truth"* (1 Kgs. 17:24). Apparently, the resuscitation of her jars and her son had been used to save the widow not just from famine but from unbelief. She too was made alive in this story. Still, why was Elijah sent to this woman? After all, she wasn't among the covenant people of God and she herself testified to her sins.

Jesus speaks of the widow in Luke 4:25–26 with these words: *"But in truth, I tell you, there were many widows in Israel in the days of Elijah, when the heavens were shut up three years and six months, and a great famine came over all the land, and Elijah was sent to none of them but only to Zarephath, in the land of Sidon, to a woman who was a widow."* God enabled a Sidonian widow to trust his Word during a period when Ahab and Israel worshipped false gods. Jesus faced unbelieving Jews in his own generation and used this story as a warning: remember, God's mercy in the past skipped over obstinate Israelites to save a Gentile. His kingdom comprises all the families of the earth (Gen. 12:3), people redeemed not by their merit or genealogy but by their faith in the Son whose death and resurrection justifies sinners. If Jesus has awakened you to new life, then may your trust in him prevail over your anxieties and encourage your obedience of his Word.

25

Jezebel and Athaliah

Dangers, toils, and snares on the path home

(1 Kings 18, 19, 21, and 2 Kings 11)

Reflection

God's purposes prevail despite the cunning enemy. The resurrection of his Son is the ultimate proof.

The Pilgrim's Progress by John Bunyan is a beautiful allegory of the Christian life. There is a scene in the book that's especially gripping. Bunyan's main character, Christian, and his companion, Faithful, travel through Vanity Fair, a market town representing worldly frivolity. The merchants of Vanity Fair observe the travelers and immediately despise them for their disinterest in their "goods." They falsely accuse the pilgrims of inciting a riot and the two are seized and beaten. The authorities hold a trial and call deceitful witnesses to testify against the men. In the end, the town will accept nothing less than the death penalty and Faithful is burned to death.[1]

Bunyan's Vanity Fair brings to mind Israel in the days of King Ahab and his wife Jezebel. Jezebel was a foreign princess, the daughter of Ethbaal (meaning "Baal is alive"). Her father was both a priest and the king of Phoenicia – which included Zarephath of Sidon.[2] The man must have been a diligent instructor of his daughter because she fiercely championed her father's gods. She incited Ahab to erect an altar to Baal and Asherah in Samaria, the capital of the northern kingdom (1 Kgs. 16:32–33; 21:25–26). Jezebel sheltered and fed at least 850 prophets of Baal and Asherah and murdered the prophets of *Yahweh* (1 Kgs. 18:4; 19:10). Elijah was among those she sought to kill (1 Kgs. 19:1–3). The narrator uses these accounts to paint Jezebel as a devious woman – yet which example could compare to the gripping tale of Naboth's vineyard?

Naboth was an Israelite with a lush vineyard adjoining Ahab's palace in Samaria. Reminiscent of David's covetous desire for his neighbor's wife (2 Sam. 11:1–27), Ahab one day cast longing eyes at his neighbor's possession. He decided that the vineyard would make a convenient vegetable garden and offered to purchase it (1 Kgs. 21:1–2). Unfortunately for Ahab, Naboth honored the Mosaic law. As the ultimate landowner, God had allotted certain plots to specific families as his divine inheritance (Josh. 13 – 21). He prohibited the transfer of property outside of families because to do so was to disinherit one's descendants from their God-given ancestral home (Lev. 25:23). For this reason, Naboth refused Ahab with these words: *"The Lord forbid that I should give you the inheritance of my fathers"* (1 Kgs. 21:3). When Jezebel heard of the matter, she was moved – not by regard for Naboth faithfulness, but by fury at his resistance. She decided to murder the man.

The queen of Israel wrote and sealed a letter in Ahab's name and sent it to the elders of Naboth's city. She detailed a chilling plot: *"Proclaim a fast, and set Naboth at the head of the people. And set two worthless men opposite him, and let them bring a charge against him, saying, 'You have cursed God and the king.' Then take him out and stone him to death"* (1 Kgs. 21:9–10). The conniving words of devious men would sanction the execution of Naboth, along with his sons, outside the city gate (2 Kgs. 9:26). Cowardly leaders feigned respect for God's name to kill a righteous man. He died for the crime of blasphemy – the very opposite of the truth. Jezebel roused Ahab to action once informed of his demise: *"Arise, take possession of the vineyard of Naboth the Jezreelite, which he refused to give you for money, for Naboth is not alive, but dead"* (1 Kgs. 21:15). Jezebel had secured the vineyard for Ahab through deceit, a practice we could trace back to the serpent in the garden.

Jezebel's hatred of God's covenant people is one example of the larger cosmic battle between the offspring of the woman and the offspring of the serpent. God put enmity between the serpent and the woman in Genesis 3:15. From here onward, Scripture unfolds the pattern of two communities: those who belong to the promised Seed of the Woman and those who are hostile to that Seed and his people. We caught sight of this enmity at the martyrdom of faithful Abel at the hands of Cain (Gen. 4:6–8). It was seen near the banks of the Nile River as Pharaoh's decree swept newborn sons of Israel away (Ex. 1:22). And this hostility would rise again to execute the descendants of King David. This time, the murderer would be Athaliah, Jezebel's daughter and pupil.

Athaliah, the daughter of Ahab and Jezebel, joined the southern kingdom of Judah as the wife of Jehoram, the son of King Jehoshaphat. Jehoram ruled Judah for only eight years and died leaving the throne to his son Ahaziah, who also died within a year (2 Chr. 22:1–9). *"When Athaliah the mother of Ahaziah saw that her son was dead, she arose and destroyed all the royal offspring"* (2 Chr. 22:10–12). Athaliah's brutality appeared to surpass even that of her mother Jezebel. She killed the Davidic line, including her own children, and held the crown for six long years. God's promise to David of offspring and a lasting kingdom seemed vanquished (2 Sam. 7:16). The serpent had landed a massive blow through this daughter of Jezebel. Still, God's purposes will always triumph in the cosmic struggle between the Seed and the snake.

Unbeknownst to Athaliah, her youngest grandson, Joash, was concealed alive. *Yahweh* preserved his people in Pharaoh's days and here too he secured a deliverer to perpetuate the line of the Savior. The boy emerged to bring Athaliah's reign to a sudden and violent end (2 Chr. 23:1–15). Even the seemingly indestructible Jezebel proved to be equally vulnerable when some servants tossed her out of a window in Jezreel and she was eaten by dogs – the very judgment foretold by Elijah (2 Kgs. 9:30–37; 1 Kgs. 21:23). God's purposes prevail despite the schemes of the cunning enemy. The resurrection of his Son, killed in the manner of Naboth, is the ultimate proof.

One dark night in Jerusalem, a man named Judas betrayed the Son of God into the hands of sinful men (Mk. 14:10–11). Worthless fellows assembled to falsely accuse Jesus (Mk. 14:55–61). He was stripped, beaten, unjustly sentenced to death, and killed outside the city gate (Mk. 15:1–37; Heb. 13:12). God's long-expected promise of a Savior seemed conquered. But three days later, Jesus emerged as the Resurrection and the Life (Jn. 11:25). He rose from the grave to crush the ancient serpent.

Apollyon, Beelzebub, the Great Dragon, Satan – the serpent's names are many, but his purpose remains the same: to wage war against the Holy One and his beloved church. Deceit is among his well-established weapons. But the risen Christ watches over his church and he will ultimately seize and hurl the Great Dragon into a pit, *"so that he might not deceive the nations any longer"* (Rev. 20:3). Until then, pilgrims can journey through Vanity Fair rooted in faith and hope. We walk through many dangers, toils, and snares, still the Savior guards his people safely home.[3]

26

The Unfaithful Wife

An atoning husband and his faithless bride

(Ezekiel 16 and Hosea 1 – 3)

Reflection

Like a faithful husband, unwilling to forsake his marriage vows, God himself atones for the sins of his faithless people.

Ezekiel 16 speaks of the birth of a child. On the day that this child was born, no one cleaned her. She was left in the filth of her afterbirth. No one swaddled her. No one fed her. She was simply cast out into the open field. She was not wanted. She was abhorred (Ezek. 16:1–5).

Yahweh passed by and saw the child wallowing in her own blood and exclaimed: "*Live!*" (Ezek. 16:6). He made her flourish like a carefully tended plant. She grew tall, strong, and beautiful. God redeemed her. He spread the edges of his garment over her and covered her nakedness. He established a covenant with her (Ezek. 16:8) God took an outcast girl left for dead and made her his own. He bent down to wash the filth of her blood. He anointed her with oil and dressed her with embroidered cloth. He covered her feet with fine leather sandals and wrapped her in linen and silk. He adorned her with gold and silver jewelry – bracelets for her wrists, a necklace around her neck, and a beautiful crown for her head. God fed her with flour, honey, and oil. The woman had no inherent beauty, but the glory given by God made her exquisite – and advanced to royalty (Ezek. 16:9–13).

The young woman's fame spread like a fragrance among the nations. But she caught a whiff of her own scent and began to glory in her splendor (Ezek. 16:14–15). She trusted her beauty above her Redeemer and used his gifts of jewelry and clothing to make idols and colorful shrines. She began to prostitute herself on these, calling out to any and every passerby who came her way. The woman became an adulterous wife, one who would rather receive strangers than her own husband (Ezek. 16:15–19). Worse still, she sacrificed her sons and daughters to her false lovers (Ezek. 16:20–21). In other words, the woman didn't remember the days of her youth, when she was wallowing, forgotten, in her own blood (Ezek. 16:22).

And who is this abandoned child turned prostitute? Ezekiel 16:1–5 identifies the woman as Jerusalem.

The author uses the art of symbolic satire to relay the origins, the apostasy, and the eventual exile of God's people. Ezekiel 16 is a stirring passage meant to be understood at two levels. First, we sense the loving husband's outrage and hurt as he confronts his adulterous and unrepentant wife. Next, we interpret the metaphoric language to understand the exact nature of God's charges against Jerusalem.[1] As we do so, we find that the plain telling of Israel's history is just as dramatic as the satire.

Once a small clan of squabbling brothers, God saw Israel and said *"Live!"* The nation grew numerous and strong and was *Yahweh's* treasured possession (Deut. 7:6). Israel conquered the land of her enemies and what nation compared with her wealth and fame in the days of King David and King Solomon (1 Kgs. 10:27)? Israel's faithful love should have been for her covenant God. Instead, she bowed down to lifeless idols and trusted in the power of foreign nations. She even burned her children in fires as offerings to Canaanite gods, following the heinous practices of the nations that God had driven out before her (2 Kgs. 16:3; 17:17; 21:6; 23:10). She didn't love *Yahweh* with all her heart, soul, and strength, and thus didn't love her neighbor as herself (Deut. 6:5). For this, the Lord removed her glory and gave her into the hands of her enemies. Like an adulterous woman, stoned in judgment, Israel was stripped bare and carried off into exile.

The northern kingdom, or Samaria, was the first to be plucked from the Promised Land. The Assyrians plundered and scattered these Israelites in 722 BC (2 Kgs. 17:6). The southern kingdom came next. Jerusalem was conquered by Babylon in 597 BC and much of its population was transported to Nebuchadnezzar's kingdom (2 Kgs. 24:8–12). In fact, the prophet Ezekiel penned his book to Israel as he sat in Babylonian captivity (Ezek. 1:1). Final destruction of Jerusalem, with a second deportation of its people, came in 586 BC (2 Kgs. 25:1–12). God's threat of exile, first cautioned by Moses, came to terrible fruition (Deut. 28:63–66). But the God who redeemed foundling Israel would not forsake her.

Years before Ezekiel's satire, a prophet to Samaria named Hosea used his marriage to a wayward woman named Gomer as an analogy of Israel's unfaithfulness to her covenant God.

We don't know much about Gomer, the daughter of Diblaim (Hos. 1:3). She is described unfalteringly as a woman who carried adultery between her breasts (Hos. 2:2). Whether she was a prostitute before her marriage to Hosea or after, Gomer left her marital bed to chase her lovers (Hos. 2:5). She bore three children whom God himself named. Any other time, this would have been an honor (2 Sam. 12:25) but Gomer's kids were together labeled "*the children of whoredom*" (Hos. 2:4). The first was named Jezreel ("a valley of judgment"), Lo-ruhama ("no mercy"), and Lo-ammi ("not my people") (Hos. 1:3–11). Israel's sin had given birth to God's judgment and these children became its symbol.

Gomer grew estranged from her husband at some point and was sold into slavery. God commanded Hosea: "*Go again, love a woman who is loved by another man and is an adulteress, even as the LORD loves the children of Israel, though they turn to other gods*" (Hos. 3:1). Hosea obeyed; he found his wife on the auction block. He purchased her for fifteen shekels of silver and some bushels of barley. And he said to her: "*You must dwell as mine for many days. You shall not play the whore, or belong to another man; so will I also be to you*" (Hos. 3:2–3). Amazingly, both the book of Hosea and Ezekiel 16 end with the hope of redemption.

Like a faithful husband, unwilling to forsake his marriage vows, God himself would atone for the sins of his idolatrous people. Ezekiel's vision for captive Israel concludes with a gracious promise: "*I will deal with you as you have done ... yet I will remember my covenant with you ... and I will establish for you an everlasting covenant ... and you shall know that I am the LORD ... when I atone for you for all that you have done*" (Ezek. 16:59–63). God would purchase his people from the slavery block of sin and establish them a new and everlasting covenant. This atonement would come ultimately through the birth of another child.

A baby was born to an impoverished young virgin (Lk. 2:1–21). Unlike Jerusalem, adorned in gold and fineries, the child Jesus didn't know earthly opulence but grew quietly in wisdom, stature, and favor with God and neighbor (Lk. 2:52). Jesus lived a life that fulfilled the sinless wholehearted devotion to God that Israel failed to offer. And yet he too was given into the hands of his enemies, stripped, and carried away to die naked for the sake of our atonement (Jn. 19:23–24).

Friends, our sins are not less than that of faithless Israel. You and I have not loved God and neighbor with all our heart, soul, and strength. For this, the shameful exposure and banishment prescribed to Israel is what we deserve. Yet even *this* humiliation, Christ has suffered on our behalf. Jesus is our atoning sacrifice (1 Jn. 2:2). He took on the sins of his bride, the church, and now adorns her with splendor beyond Ezekiel 16 – the gift of his own righteousness. You and I have no inherent beauty, but the glory of the risen Christ makes us exquisite. Pray for the grace to love this Bridegroom of your atonement with wholehearted devotion.

27

Esther

Feasting awaits those who hunger for joy

(Esther 1 – 10)

Reflection

Relief would have come for the Jews, even if Esther remained silent – because God's faithfulness, and not Esther's courage, was their true help.

Earthly kingdoms – however great they may be – don't last forever. So, the Babylonians who captured Jerusalem in our last chapter were themselves conquered by the Persians in 539 BC. The prophet Jeremiah foretold a Jewish return to the Promised Land after seventy years of captivity (Jer. 25:12). God fulfilled this word through Cyrus the Great of Persia. Cyrus made an incredible proclamation shortly after his conquest of Babylon: *"The LORD, the God of heaven ... has charged me to build him a house at Jerusalem, which is in Judah. Whoever is among you of all his people, may his God be with him, and let him go up to Jerusalem, which is in Judah, and rebuild the house of the LORD"* (Ezra 1:2–3). Many

Jews returned – but others remained scattered throughout the Persian Empire.[1] Esther was one of these. The biblical narrative that bears her name uses the contrasting themes of obedience and disobedience, perceived power and absolute power, and plot reversals to remind Israel of *Yahweh's* covenant faithfulness in a dark and distant land.

The narrative is set in Susa during the days of King Ahasuerus (also known as Xerxes). Xerxes' empire was vast, comprising over 127 provinces (Esth. 1:1–2). The story opens with a grand feast meant to display the *"riches of his royal glory and the splendor and pomp of his greatness for many days, 180 days"* (Esth. 1:4). From the palace curtains to the pillars, to gold and silver couches, to the free-flowing wine, the narrator captures the king's ostentatious grandeur in detail. We can't question Xerxes' wealth in Esther 1:1–9. However, we doubt the extent of his power in the rest of the chapter.

Xerxes decided to conclude his feast by displaying another "trophy" of sorts: his wife. He ordered seven eunuchs *"to bring Queen Vashti before the king with her royal crown, in order to show the peoples and the princes her beauty, for she was lovely to look at"* (Esth. 1:11). Vashti refused to appear. The narrator skips past the reason for her refusal and focuses instead on the king's reaction. Xerxes is pictured throwing a temper tantrum (Esth. 1:12). Like a big bad wolf – intimidating but ultimately weak – the king huffed and puffed but couldn't make Vashti obey. His court officials rushed to control public opinion, and their own wives. They suggested an irrevocable edict – the first of several edicts that drive the plotline of this narrative. Every man in the kingdom was ordered to be: *"master in his own household"* (Esth. 1:19–22). But apparently, this was something the king himself was not.

The officials suggested a second decree: *"let the king appoint officers in all the provinces of his kingdom to gather all the beautiful young virgins to the harem in Susa ... Let their cosmetics be given them. And let the young woman who pleases the king be queen instead of Vashti"* (Esth. 2:2–4). Xerxes' marital issues exploded into a case of exploitation as officers seized the daughters of Susa for his personal use.[2] Esther was among the virgins taken. She became one of hundreds in Xerxes' harem. Still, the narrator never loses track of Esther – she is set apart from the crowd in various ways.

First, Esther is identified to the reader as the orphaned Hadassah, the cousin of Mordecai the Jew. Mordecai was a Benjaminite from King Saul's lineage. He was among the Jews deported to Babylon at the fall of Jerusalem (Esth. 2:5–6). He now served at the king's gate in Susa and cared for Esther as his own daughter (Esth. 3:1–3; 2:7). The younger Esther may have grown up in exile with no direct knowledge of the Promised Land. As a young child, I moved to the United States from Ghana and can confess to the blurred allegiances of a person formed by two cultures. Was this Esther's experience in Susa? We don't have the benefit of her views, or her thoughts as officers led her to the king's harem. We only know this: Esther went to the palace determined to obey Mordecai from afar. She kept her Jewish ancestry a secret *"for Mordecai had commanded her not to make it known"* (Esth. 2:10). The Jewish orphan presented as a Persian maiden and won the favor of the king.

Xerxes loved Esther more than all the virgins, and *"set the royal crown on her head and made her queen instead of Vashti"* (Esth. 2:17). A descendant of King Saul became royalty in an empire full of enemies. The sudden emergence of a dubious new character in this story will emphasize the dangers posed to God's exilic community in this era.

King Xerxes promoted *"Haman the Agagite, the son of Hammedatha, and advanced him and set his throne above all the officials who were with him"* (Esth. 3:1). Haman's promotion came with an interesting bonus: Xerxes ordered everyone who served at his gate to bow down in homage to the man. The king's words were absolute, yet, for the second time in this narrative, someone chose to ignore Xerxes. Mordecai did not bow down or pay homage to Haman (Esth. 3:2–4).

This Haman, like Esther and Mordecai, was the descendant of an ancient king – his forefather was the Amalekite ruler, Agag. The Amalekites had opposed Israel following the Exodus and the Lord ordered

King Saul to destroy them and all their property (1 Sam. 15:1–3). Saul vacillated in his obedience, he reserved some plunder and kept Agag alive. He treated *Yahweh* like a human king whose command might be tossed aside. God tore the kingdom from Saul for this sin and the prophet Samuel completed Saul's abandoned task by hacking Agag to pieces (1 Sam. 15:17–35).

Now it seemed Saul and Agag were again facing each other through their progeny. Mordecai would honor *Yahweh* this time without fail. He chose to recognize God's judgment against the Amalekites over Xerxes' command to honor Haman.

"And when Haman saw that Mordecai did not bow down or pay homage to him, Haman was filled with fury" (Esth. 3:5). Haman began to plot his revenge, but not against Mordecai alone. Haman wanted the slaughter of every Jew throughout the Persian Empire. Israel had nearly demolished the Amalekites in Saul's day, now an Amalekite descendant was scheming to destroy Israel. Haman manipulated gullible King Xerxes into signing a third edict – this one called for the murder and plunder of *"all Jews, young and old, women and children, in one day, the thirteenth day of the twelfth month, which is the month of Adar"* (Esth. 3:13). The genocidal spirit seen in Athaliah (2 Kgs. 11), Pharaoh (Ex. 1), and ultimately the seed of the serpent (Gen. 3:15) was poised for its deadliest strike yet. God's people were spread across a pagan kingdom and *Yahweh's* long-ago promise of a Savior appeared distant and elusive. Would exiled Israel die – and with her, the hope of the redeeming Seed?

Mordecai tore his clothes, put on sackcloth and ashes, and hit the streets of Susa with loud cries (Esth. 4:1). Esther heard of his mourning and sent a servant to inquire. Mordecai responded with a copy of the death decree and a command to the queen that she should *"go to the king to beg his favor and plead with him on behalf of her people"* (Esth. 4:8). Esther didn't argue with his order to disclose her Jewish identity. However, this woman who had always obeyed Mordecai now hesitated to comply with his full request. She explained: *"if any man or woman goes to the king inside the inner court without being called, there is but one law – to be put to death, except the one to whom the king holds out the golden scepter so that he may live"* (Esth. 4:11). Xerxes had punished Queen Vashti for refusing to come when called. Conversely, he could kill Queen Esther for appearing without a summons. It seemed safer for her to abide by the king's rules and remain silent. Mordecai disagreed. He sent this reply:

> *Do not think to yourself that in the king's palace you will escape any more than all the other Jews. For if you keep silent at this time, relief and deliverance will rise for the Jews from another place, but you and your father's house will perish. And who knows whether you have not come to the kingdom for such a time as this?* (Esth. 4:13–14).

There was a King higher than Xerxes whose decrees were truly irrevocable. This King had pledged himself to Israel, and for that reason, relief and deliverance were certain for the Jews. This meant that Esther's security didn't rest in Xerxes' laws or palace – but in her place among God's covenant people. The truth of Mordecai's words seemed to convince Esther. She asked the exilic community of Susa to pray and fast with her for three days. Their grief and hunger stand in contrast to the joy and feasting that begins and ends this narrative. Israel's survival was on the line and Esther prayed for help to be her willing mediator. She would face King Xerxes – and if she perished, she perished (Esth. 4:16).

Esther went before Xerxes without a summons. She disobeyed the king – as Vashti had done – yet a golden scepter was held out to her (Esth. 5:1–3). She invited Xerxes and Haman to a feast. Perhaps it was known that alcohol, mixed with bad news, fueled Xerxes' tantrums because Esther waited for the wine to flow on the second day of feasting before revealing her ancestry and exposing Haman's wicked conspiracy against her people (Esth. 7:1–6). Haman was immediately sentenced to death and was hung on the very gallows he had prepared for Mordecai the previous day (Esth. 7:7–10; 5:9–14).

Xerxes sanctioned a parallel decree allowing the Jews to defend themselves on the thirteenth day of Adar. They were permitted to *"destroy, to kill, and to annihilate any armed force of any people or province that might attack them, children and women included, and to plunder their goods"* (Esth. 8:11). The exiles would kill thousands of opponents throughout the Persian Empire, including the ten sons of Haman (Esth. 9:12). These Agagites were devoted to destruction, as *Yahweh* had commanded centuries before. And in contrast to Saul, who disobeyed the Lord for the sake of spoils (1 Sam. 15:20–23), the Jews in Esther day didn't touch the plunder of their enemies (Esth. 9:10, 15, 16). They stopped short of Xerxes' edict, in view of a higher King.

God's name isn't mentioned in the book of Esther. There's no prophet of the Lord with an explicit word of comfort and assurance for the exiled Jews. Yet God isn't absent. He sits as the King with absolute power – the one who rules, not by the counsel of cunning men but by the wisdom of his own will (Eph. 1:11). He providentially ordained the structures of an earthly court within human history to position his chosen mediator and bring about salvation for his people.[3] God's promised Savior would come as an obedient Mediator, greater than Esther. Israel's Persian queen didn't perish in her act of mediation – but Christ would. He takes the death sentence due to his people and resurrects to usher them to God's throne without the fear of judgment. You can trust and obey Jesus in a world where God's promises often feel distant and elusive. Know that feasting awaits us who grieve today and hunger for eternal joy in God's presence.

PART SIX:

Women Between the Testaments to Christ

28

Elizabeth

A hope deferred is not always denied

(Luke 1)

Reflection

Even when our hopes and prayers seem deferred, God is still working through his Word and Spirit to display his faithfulness to his covenant people.

Israel is a dispersed diaspora by the end of the Old Testament. We observed in the book of Esther that, while a remnant of Jews returned to Judah, many lived scattered throughout the Persian Empire (Esth. 3:6). They remained within the broader diaspora as empires changed from one power to another. First came Alexander the Great's Greek Empire in the late fourth century BC, then Egypt and Syria, and eventually the Roman Empire in the first century BC.[1] Judah remained subjugated in all these changes. The vast and prosperous nation that existed in the days of King David and Solomon was gone.

God sent a few post-exilic prophets, like Haggai and Malachi, to encourage a remnant Israel but these voices didn't remain. Silence followed Malachi for four hundred long years. Scholars call this time the Intertestamental Period. God's people were chastened for their shameless apostasy – yet they lived with expectancy. If God's promised judgment had proven true, then surely his covenant vows of salvation to their forefathers would also be fulfilled. God's faithfulness was Israel's hope as she lingered in somber silence. As we pass from the end of the Old Testament to the Gospels, we find a sunrise dawning on those waiting in darkness (Lk. 1:78–79).

A Gentile physician living in the Roman Empire – a meticulous historian named Luke – penned a detailed account of the life and works of Jesus Christ. His purpose for writing was to give his audience certainty of the things they had learned about Christ (Lk. 1:1–4). Luke's work begins with the unusual birth story of a man named John. John's coming ended the four hundred years of prophetic silence. God was sending a herald to prepare Israel for his most astounding work in salvation history. The account begins with an elderly couple – Elizabeth and Zechariah.

Elizabeth and Zechariah lived in the days of Herod the Great (Lk. 1:5). This man sat on a throne in Judea, but he was no son of David. Herod was a wealthy Edomite appointed ruler by the Romans.[2] The ruthless puppet-king was another reminder of the judgment Israel suffered for her rebellion. Elizabeth and Zechariah, who lived in the hill country of Judah (Lk. 1:39), would have rejected the idea of Herod as their true king. Perhaps they prayed regularly for the birth of the Davidic King whose reign would never end (2 Sam. 7:11–13).

Elizabeth and Zechariah were both descendants of Aaron, from the tribe of Levi. The author of the book of Luke describes them as *"righteous before God, walking blamelessly in all the commandments and statutes of the Lord"* (Lk. 1:6). Contrary to some of the Levites encountered in the Old Testament (Judg. 19:1; 1 Sam. 1:2), Zechariah obeyed the Mosaic law in choosing his wife. He married one woman, a daughter of Aaron from among his own people (Lk. 1:5; Lev. 21:14). One might assume that this righteous couple would have known the joy of every blessing – yet *"they had no child, because Elizabeth was barren, and both were advanced in years"* (Lk. 1:7).

How many years had the two prayed for the gift of a child? How did Zechariah bear the disappointment of this deferred hope? How did Elizabeth manage the reproachful remarks of family and neighbors who viewed their childlessness as *her* shame (Lk. 1:25)? Whatever the answers, the couple had maintained a long holy life without children, without new revelation from God, and under a brutal Roman Empire with its false Judean king. God would work within all these circumstances to display his faithfulness to Elizabeth and Zechariah – and to his covenant people.

Zechariah was a priest of the division of Abijah (Lk. 1:5). King David had long ago organized the sons of Aaron into twenty-four priestly divisions, with Abijah at number eight (1 Chr. 24:1–19). While his division was serving at the temple before God, Zechariah *"was chosen by lot to enter the temple of the Lord and burn incense"* (Lk. 1:8–9). Fragrant incense, representing prayer, burned on the altar in front of the veil that separated the Holy Place from the Most Holy Place (Ex. 30:1–8). Descendants of Aaron were to offer fresh incense twice daily, morning and evening, and so keep the smoke rising perpetually. According to one commentary, "priests who had never offered incense would cast lots to see who would take the turn … we're to imagine that Zechariah, the righteous, aging priest, had been waiting for the lot to fall on him for years, probably just as long as he had been waiting for a child."[3] The lot was cast and, on this occasion, it pleased the Lord to appoint Zechariah to the assignment.

Zechariah's heart must have pounded as he entered the Holy Place. The altar of incense was before him, just steps away from the Most Holy Place where the Ark of the Covenant, the symbol of God's presence, rested. A congregation of priests and worshipers were assembled outside in prayer (Lk. 1:10). Zechariah would burn incense and then leave to pronounce a benediction on the people. His task was important, but not long. Unbeknownst to the priest, however, God was planning to detain him in conversation (Lk. 1:21). The angel Gabriel appeared *"standing on the right side of the altar of incense. And Zechariah was troubled when he saw him, and fear fell upon him"* (Lk. 1:11–12).

Gabriel comforted the shaken priest before delivering astonishing news: God had heard his prayers. Elizabeth would have a son; he was to be named John (Lk. 1:13). Like Hannah, the baby born to Elizabeth would be devoted to the Lord from childhood (1 Sam. 1:11). God was answering their prayers. Still, Gabriel's words stretched beyond the house of Zechariah to the entire house of Israel. *Yahweh* was fulfilling Malachi's prophecy (Mal. 4:5–6), an Elijah-like prophet was coming into the world to *"turn the hearts of the fathers to the children, and the disobedient to the wisdom of the just, to make ready for the Lord a people prepared"* (Lk. 1:13–17). Elizbeth and Zechariah's son would be a forerunner to the promised Savior. Like incense rising perpetually before the Lord, Israel's prayers for salvation had been heard and now answered.

Gabriel's staggering message should have brought joy – not doubts. Yet Zechariah seemed unsure. The priest alluded to Abraham's words from Genesis 15:8: *"How shall I know this? For I am an old man, and my wife is advanced in years."* Abraham believed God's promises and then asked a question of how; God assured him with a covenant agreement (Gen. 15:6–20). Zechariah, on the other hand, interrogated Gabriel in disbelief – so God gave the doubting priest a sign of his own: *"behold, you will be silent and unable to speak until the day that these things take place, because you did not believe my words, which will be fulfilled in their time"* (Lk. 1:20). Zechariah emerged mute from the Holy Place, completed his week of duties, and returned home to a wife who would soon conceive a son (Lk. 1:22–24).

Elizabeth woke up one day to discover that she was pregnant. I remember my first pregnancy after several years of trying for a baby.

My joy was inexpressible. I can't imagine Elizabeth's feelings. Decades of longing and prayer and then this ... the conception of a child in her old age. The Lord had removed her reproach among the people (Lk. 1:25). Still, Elizabeth hid herself for five months (Lk. 1:24). We're not given a reason, but the decision must have filled her world with silence. Her husband was voiceless, and family and neighbors were unseen. Elizabeth spent her first two trimesters in quiet expectation. Perhaps the Gospel writer meant to give us a picture of Israel's own waiting in silence for the fulfillment of God's promise.

This drought of words ended in Elizabeth's sixth month. Her cousin Mary entered her house with a greeting that sent her baby leaping in utero. Elizabeth, filled with God's Spirit, exclaimed with a loud cry: *"Blessed are you among women, and blessed is the fruit of your womb! And why is this granted to me that the mother of my Lord should come to me? For behold, when the sound of your greeting came to my ears, the baby in my womb leaped for joy"* (Lk. 1:41–45). Mary had conceived the incarnate Son of God, an embryo – probably no larger than a poppy seed yet – the object of praise! Mary sang a song that must have felt to Elizabeth like a shower of words after months of famine (Lk. 1:46–55).

Zechariah joined the singing at the birth and naming of their son, John. For nine months, the old man used a writing tablet for communication (Lk. 1:63). He must have scribbled Gabriel's message down for Elizabeth because the new mother insisted on the name John for her son (Lk. 1:59–60). Zechariah's tongue was loosened as he confirmed this name in writing. He immediately pronounced a benediction, the very act that should have followed his incense burning months earlier. The old priest blessed God for his covenant faithfulness to Abraham in sending salvation from the house of David (Lk. 1:67–79). The long-expected Seed was coming to light the darkness!

Christ's church today, like Elizabeth and Zechariah, is in places where brutal earthly rulers govern. There is no new revelation for us from God; the canon of Scripture is closed because the Father has spoken to us by his Son and no new revelation is needed (Heb. 1:1–2). God is working through his Word and Spirit within our times to display his faithfulness to his covenant people. Even if our hopes and prayers seem deferred, let us live holy lives that trust God's revealed Word, spoken to us by Jesus, as we wait for the promised second coming of our Savior.

29

Mary

God exalts the poor in spirit

(Luke 1 – 2)

Reflection

Mary's Son is our unique Savior. He is the God-man who is qualified to represent humanity before God and the only One who can earn for us the righteousness required for our justification.

The angel Gabriel was sent to a city of Galilee named Nazareth during Elizabeth's sixth month of pregnancy. The town was a commonplace village 70 miles north of Jerusalem.[1] It didn't have a good reputation (Jn. 1:46; 7:52). One commentary explains that "While Galileans were despised by Judeans, Galileans themselves despised people from Nazareth."[2] The place is mentioned nowhere in the Hebrew Scriptures, it appeared to be an insignificant village without prophetic importance. God chose *this* town for his Son. He sent a glorious messenger, down to earth, to the poor obscure home of a virgin, the lowliest of maidens, the betrothed of a simple carpenter named Joseph (Mt. 1:18).[3] This young woman, Mary, would be the mother of the long-expected promised Savior.

Gabriel began with an address that puzzled Mary: *"Greetings, O favored one, the Lord is with you"* (Lk. 1:28). The girl, perhaps a teen, seemed like a deep thinker. She was likely frightened by the appearance of the angel – and yet she found the capacity to chew on his words, trying to discern their meaning (Lk. 1:29). However, Mary wouldn't get far before Gabriel would give her more to consider:

> *Do not be afraid, Mary, for you have found favor with God. And behold, you will conceive in your womb and bear a son, and you shall call his name Jesus. He will be great and will be called the Son of the Most High. And the Lord God will give to him the throne of his father David, and he will reign over the house of Jacob forever, and of his kingdom there will be no end* (Lk. 1:30–33).

Young Mary was familiar with the Hebrew Scriptures (her later song in Elizabeth's home will prove this). She knew that women before her had conceived children foretold by God. Isaac had been announced to Sarah in Genesis 18:10 and Rebekah was told of Jacob and Esau in Genesis 25:23. Other women, like Jochebed and Hannah, had mothered divinely ordained mediators – like Moses and Samuel (Ex. 2:1–10; 1 Sam. 1:24–28). From the *protoevangelion* (the first gospel announcement in Genesis 3:15) onward, women in Israel had been the bearers of a glorious nation. Yet which of them had ever heard the words now spoken to Mary by the angel Gabriel? Her child would be called the Son of the Most High!

A girl living in a Roman occupied village in the first century BC would conceive the eternal King. Mary's Son would hold Judah's scepter and reign over the house of Jacob (Gen. 49:10). God would give him the promised throne of his father David. There hadn't been a king on David's throne since Zedekiah was dragged by King Nebuchadnezzar to Babylon at the siege of Jerusalem (2 Kgs. 25:1–12). Yet God *had* promised David an offspring with an everlasting kingdom (2 Sam. 7:11–13). According to Gabriel's message, that King would soon be born of Mary. The young woman pondered this astonishing news, then posed a question: *"How will this be, since I am a virgin?"* (Lk. 1:34). Gabriel's answer would further set Mary apart from every other mother in human history. *"The Holy Spirit will come upon you, and the power of the Most High will overshadow you; therefore the child to be born will be called holy – the Son of God"* (Lk. 1:35).

Mary's firstborn child wouldn't come by natural means. The Holy Spirit would overshadow the virgin, as he had done over the face of the earth at the beginning (Gen. 1:2). She wouldn't conceive by sexual intercourse. Rather, the baby born of Mary would be generated by the Spirit of God. The child would be a unique God-man: one born of woman and thus fully human *and* conceived by the power of the Holy Spirit and therefore fully God. Gabriel called his name Jesus, meaning "*Yahweh* is salvation." Jesus' nature makes him a unique Savior: as a human being, he is *qualified* to serve as the representative Head of humanity. And as the divine Son of God – free from original sin – Jesus alone *can* earn for us the righteousness required for our justification (Rom. 5:18–19).[4] He's the Second Adam able to crush the curse brought on by our first father. He is the Seed of the Woman, the hope of Eve (Gen. 3:15). And he's also the Son of lowly Mary from Nazareth.

The girl heard Gabriel's words and then replied: *"Behold, I am the servant of the Lord; let it be to me according to your word"* (Lk. 1:38). Mary submitted fully to God's will and answered the angel with the unwavering trust old Zechariah had failed to show (Lk. 1:18). Satisfied, Gabriel departed from her (Lk. 1:38). Mary wasn't far behind to leave herself. The angel had slipped in the news of another pregnancy in his message to her. Her relative Elizabeth, Zechariah's aging wife, long believed to be barren, had conceived a son and was now in her sixth month of pregnancy (Lk. 1:36–37). God had done what seemed impossible!

Mary arose and went with haste into the hill country of Judah (Lk. 1:39). She entered Elizabeth's home with a greeting that caught the ear of the old woman *and* the baby in her womb. The six-month-old fetus rejoiced in utero at the sound of Mary's words and Elizabeth, filled with the Holy Spirit, raised her voice and prophesied:

> *Blessed are you among women, and blessed is the fruit of your womb! And why is this granted to me that the mother of my Lord should come to me? ... And blessed is she who believed that there would be a fulfillment of what was spoken to her from the Lord* (Lk. 1:42–45).

Four hundred years of prophetic silence ended in the courtyard of Zechariah's house as Elizabeth blessed Mary *and* her unborn son: somewhere between Gabriel's departure and her arrival in the hill country of Judah, Mary had conceived Jesus. The promised Savior would come within months!

Perhaps Elizabeth's blessing was Mary's first indication of her pregnancy. God didn't waste any time in fulfilling his word through Gabriel. Mary lifted her voice in song. Her Magnificat, which alludes to Hannah's 1 Samuel 2 prayer, is a boast of the God who regards the lowly above the proud (Lk. 1:46–55). Mary's spirit rejoiced in her Savior, the God who scatters the mighty but exalts the humble. Human wisdom would have painted the mother of Christ as wealthy and prestigious. Instead, we find a seemingly insignificant girl from a despised village. Yet God's choice of Mary reflects the general pattern of the One who chooses the obscure for his work in salvation. Mary reminds us of Israel herself – the nameless nation God called to produce a Savior into the world. *Yahweh* remembered his covenant promises to his servant Israel and birthed the long-expected Seed of the Woman through a poor girl, made rich by his grace.

The word "favor" in Gabriel's Luke 1:28 greeting is rendered "full of grace." The term signifies that Mary was a recipient (and not a source) of grace.[5] God used this faithful woman in a unique way in salvation history and for that, all generations will call her blessed (Lk. 1:48). Yet Mary's Son extends glorious grace today to *all* who trust in him (Eph. 1:6). You and I can magnify God with Mary for the humble Jesus who lived and died for our sake as a poor man from Nazareth – but was resurrected as the eternal King on David's throne. Those who recognize their spiritual poverty enough to hunger after Christ will be lifted to reign with him (Mt. 5:3). In Jesus, Mary's Son, we can see that *"God chose what is low and despised in the world, even things that are not, to bring to nothing things that are, so that no human being might boast in the presence of God"* (1 Cor. 1:28–29).

30

Christ, the Seed of the Woman

He will not forget you

Reflection

Yahweh Elohim didn't forsake the women of Scripture – nor did he forget his gracious poem in the garden. The Snake-Crusher came to make his blessings flow, wherever the curse is found.

I delivered a beautiful baby girl one July midnight and brought her home. I soon discovered that midnight (and later) was in fact her preferred social hour. For *months*, my sweet infant struggled to rest at night. My deepest slumber was no match for her nighttime cries. No amount of exhaustion could overcome them. She called out and I awoke. This meant that I was often pacing or rocking a baby in pitch darkness.

On one such occasion, as I attempted to lull my daughter back to sleep, I wondered if God noticed his children the way I heard my child's cries. Did our tears grip his attention in a similar manner? This midnight scene in my baby's room seemed a fitting analogy for God's own care for his people. But for some reason, I couldn't think of the Scripture to settle this as truth in my mind. So, I let the thought go and proceeded to rock my child. An hour later, dizzy with tiredness, and still holding a restless baby, I decided it was time to quit. The loving momma had hit the wall. I placed my daughter back into her crib and slipped out – thankfully, she made no noise. As my head hit my own pillow, a thought jumped to my mind: my expressions of love for my baby, while there might be some parallel, are microscopic compared to God's love for his children. The scale is simply not the same.

As much as I love my children, I'm also weak: I fail, I tire, and I even give up. But God is God. He is more than able and lacks for nothing. He never leaves nor forsakes his own. I adjusted my perspective on God's love – and just as sleep came to silence these thoughts, the Scripture I had hoped for earlier suddenly came: *"Can a mother forget the baby at her breast and have no compassion on the child she has borne? Though she may forget, I will not forget you"* (Is. 49:15, NIV). *Yahweh Elohim*, the covenant-keeping Lord God of Israel, does not forget his children. We have seen this truth on our tour across the Old Testament.

Our journey began with a Creator God (Gen. 1:27). The transcendent God who acted alone in Genesis 1 is also the omnipresent, personal Lord God who initiated relationship with his created beings in Genesis 2. This God clothed a depraved Eve and inserted her into this glorious drama of redemption. She would be the mother of the living and would generate a distant Seed to crush the head of the serpent (Gen. 3:15–16, 21). Next, we met suffering, yet hopeful, mothers in Genesis. The deception that began in Eden crept into their families – but God's promises were not overcome by the sins of these matriarchs. The Abrahamic promises of land and seed were passed from Sarah's son Isaac to Rebekah's son Jacob, to Leah's son Judah, and so on until Israel was no longer a small band of brothers but a strong and fruitful nation (Gen. 12:1–3; Ex. 1:6–7).

By now God's people were enslaved in Egypt but *Yahweh* never forget his children. He used women like Shiphrah, Puah, Jochebed, and Miriam to show a serpentine pharaoh that his purposes cannot be thwarted – and in fact, they often shine brightest in the shadow of opposing enemies (Ex. 15:1–21). God preserved Moses through the efforts of these women and used him to mediate a glorious victory over Pharoah and to sanctify his covenant people to dwell with their God in holiness (Ex. 19 – 24). Sin would keep Moses and his generation from the Promised Land, but God doesn't forget Israel. He used Moses' servant Joshua to plant a young nation in a land rich with milk and honey (Josh. 1:1–9). Israel should have grown strong in faith in this soil, instead, she became a wild vine (Jer. 2:21).

The generations after Joshua provoked God's anger by turning away to the gods of Canaan (Judg. 2:11–20). *Yahweh* strengthened Israel's adversaries against her until she cried out in repentance and found his mercy. It was within this cycle of apostasy, judgment, and deliverance that we met women like Deborah, Jael, and the Levite's unnamed concubine. God's Genesis 3:15 promise of salvation appeared somewhat distant from the perspective of their dark narratives. Still, *Yahweh*'s Word prevailed in the period of the judges. In these days when there was no king and everyone did what was right in their own eyes (Judg. 21:25), *Yahweh* displayed his *hesed*, his loving-kindness, by redeeming a Moabite woman named Ruth to generate future kings who would continue the line to his promised Seed. Ruth's son Obed became the grandfather of Israel's King David (Ruth 4:18–22). The nation would move from a judiciary to a monarchy.

Israel crowned the kings anticipated in the book of Judges. Yet, the nation had never been without a Sovereign – she simply chose self-autonomy rather than devotion to *Yahweh* (1 Sam. 8:7–9). God enthroned David and promised him an offspring with an everlasting crown (2 Sam. 7:11–13). David was a man after God's heart yet even he failed to embody the vision of the king who *"dawns on [his people] like the morning light"* (2 Sam. 23:4). Bathsheba, Tamar, and Rizpah could testify to that.

David's son Solomon turned to idolatry and God's judgment brought a divided Israel (1 Kgs. 12:1–24). The southern kingdom, led by Davidic kings, comprised Judah and Benjamin and the northern kingdom, led by apostate kings like Ahab, held the remaining ten. Both kingdoms proved faithless in the end (Ezek. 16; Hos. 1:2–3). They didn't love *Yahweh* or neighbor (Deut. 6:5). We have accounts of gross immorality, violence, and vile injustice in both nations (2 Kgs. 21:16; Ezek. 22). For this, God gave his people into the hands of their enemies to be exiled. Assyria plucked the northern kingdom from their land in 722 BC (2 Kgs. 17:6). And final destruction and deportation of Judah by Babylon came in 586 BC (2 Kgs. 25:1–12). Israel's glory was gone, yet God did not forget her.

God raised up Cyrus the Great of Persia to conquer Babylon. A remnant of Jews returned to Judah under Cyrus to rebuild a second temple (Ezra 1:1–5). But centuries later, many, like Esther, remained scattered throughout the Persian Empire. When genocide threatened to annihilate the Jews, God's providential hand positioned Esther as queen for the salvation for his people (Esth. 4:13–14). Many Jews remained within the broader diaspora as empires changed from one power to another. God sent a few post-exilic prophets, like Haggai and Malachi, to encourage a remnant Israel, but these voices didn't remain. Silence followed Malachi for four hundred long years. Israel sat subdued yet expectant. If God's promised judgment had proven true, then surely his covenant vows of salvation to their forefathers would also be fulfilled.

We enter Roman occupied first century BC from the Old Testament to find two pregnant women united in worship. One is elderly Elizabeth and the other is the virgin Mary (Lk. 1:39–56). The famine of prophetic revelation had ended. Elizabeth's son, John was coming to prepare Israel for her Savior, Jesus – the son of Mary (Mal. 4:5–6; Lk. 1:13–17). The long-expected Seed of the Woman would soon be born. *Yahweh Elohim* didn't forget his children. He sent the promised Son of David, the King who is light to those who sit in darkness (Lk. 1:32, 78–79).

The Old Testament Scriptures move historically and chronologically forward to reveal God's salvation of sinners through the person and work of Jesus Christ. Our journey has revealed a saving God who sees and hears his own. Eve and her daughters who follow her in Scripture suffered in many ways – but God drew near to help them. He didn't forget these women – nor did he forget his gracious poem in the garden (Gen. 3:15). The Snake-Crusher came to make his blessings flow, wherever the curse is found. And God was pleased to use weak women to birth him.

Women are featured in the story of redemption as you continue deeper into the New Testament. You will find that Jesus doesn't forget them in his earthly ministry.[1] He healed them (Lk. 13:10–17; Mt. 9:20–22); interacted with them (Mk. 7:24–30; Jn. 4:1–45); received their care (Mt. 26:6–13; Lk. 8:2–3; 10:40); and welcomed them as his followers and witnesses (Mt. 28:5–8; Jn. 20:1–2). The ascended Christ empowered women of the first century church to labor in the gospel. Romans 16 provides a glimpse of the early church and the shared mission of its men and women. The Apostle Paul names nine sisters in that chapter, a few commended for their hard work include Persis, whom he calls a "beloved"; Junia who suffered as a fellow prisoner; and fellow workers Prisca and Phoebe. In both the Old and New Testament Scriptures, we see that God doesn't forget women. Their names and accounts are part of the biggest story ever told – a story meant to point us to Jesus.

God's plan of final salvation is still unfolding as his church today anticipates the return of Christ. We are women who live east of Eden in a post-Genesis 3 world. We are surrounded by anxiety, ambiguity, and abuse. We too are the daughters of Eve. We yearn for the Seed of the Woman to come and strike sin and Satan with a last fatal blow (Rev. 21:4). As we wait, we know that *Yahweh Elohim* will not forget us. He never leaves nor forsakes his children (Is. 49:15). Every promise given to his church finds its "Yes" in Christ (2 Cor. 1:20). He hears and sees you – and your life of faith is part of the biggest story ever told. So point to Christ as the center of your certain hope as you labor for his glory.

Notes

Part One: Creation, Fall, the Promised Seed, and Eve

1. Creation

1. Nielson, K., *Women and God: Hard Questions, Beautiful Truth* (The Good Book Company, 2018), 17.
2. Ryken, L., and P.G. Ryken, eds., *The Literary Study Bible: English Standard Version* (Wheaton, IL: Crossway Bibles, 2007), 5.
3. Sproul, R.C., *Everyone's a Theologian: An Introduction to Systematic Theology* (Orlando, FL: Reformation Trust, 2014), 100.

2. The Fall and the Seed

1. Sproul, *Everyone's a Theologian*, 104–105.
2. Sproul, *Everyone's a Theologian*, 108.

3. Eve

1. Sproul, R.C., ed. *The Reformation Study Bible: English Standard Version* (Orlando, FL: Reformation Trust, 2015), 20.
2. Ryken and Ryken, *Literary Study Bible: ESV*, 8–9.
3. Challies, T., "Pain in Childbearing" *Challies*, May 12, 2011, https://www.challies.com/articles/pain-in-childbearing/, accessed December 17, 2020.
4. Ross, A.P., *Creation and Blessing: A Guide to the Study and Exposition of Genesis* (Grand Rapids, MI: Baker Academic, 1998), 158.
5. Sproul, *Reformation Study Bible: ESV*, 21.

Part Two: Women of Genesis

4. Sarah

1. Sarah was ten years younger than Abram. She is sixty-five years old in Genesis 12:4 and dies at the age of 127 in Genesis 23:1.
2. Duke, A., J. Hamilton and S. Emadi, "Genesis 15 – 17: On the Lord's Covenant Ceremony, Sarah's Covenant Scheme, and Abraham's Covenant Sign (Bible Talk Ep. 5)" *Bible Talk* podcast, October 7, 2020, https://www.9marks.org/conversations/genesis-15-17-on-the-lords-covenant-ceremony-sarahs-covenant-scheme-and-abrahams-covenant-sign-bible-talk-ep-5/, accessed October 22, 2021.
3. "Abram, an ancient West Semitic name, means 'exalted father'... 'Abraham' sounds like a Hebrew expression meaning 'father of a multitude of nations.' His old name spoke of his [exalted father, Trah], his new name speaks of his many offspring.... Both [Sarai and Sarah] seem to be variants meaning 'princess.' Her birth name probably looks back on her noble descent, whereas her covenant name looks ahead to her noble descendants." Sproul, *Reformation Study Bible: ESV*, 39-40

5. Hagar

1. Sproul, *Reformation Study Bible: ESV*, 38.

7. Rachel

1. MacArthur, J., ed. *The MacArthur Study Bible* (Wheaton, IL: Crossway Bibles, 2010), 58.
2. It is during this trip that God changed Jacob's name to Israel (see Gen. 32:22–32).
3. MacArthur, *The MacArthur Study Bible*, 60.

8. Leah

1. Duke, A., J. Hamilton and S. Emadi, "Genesis 29 – 31: On Rachel's Junk Science, Jacob's Ancient Eugenics, and the Fear of Isaac's Unshakeable Sovereignty (Bible Talk Ep. 10)" *Bible Talk* podcast, November 11, 2020, https://www.9marks.org/conversations/genesis-29-31-on-rachels-junk-science-

jacobs-ancient-eugenics-and-the-fear-of-isaacs-unshakeable-sovereignty-bible-talk-ep-10/, accessed October 22, 2021.

2. Ross, *Creation and Blessing*, 509–510.

9. Tamar

1. Sproul, *Reformation Study Bible: ESV*, 74.
2. Bruno, C., J. Compton and K. McFadden, *Biblical Theology According to the Apostle: How the Earliest Christians Told the Story of Israel* (Downers Grove, Il: IVP Academic, 2020), 18.

Part Three: Women of the Exodus

10. Shiphrah and Puah

1. Duke, A., J. Hamilton, and S. Emadi, "Exodus 1 – 2: On Moses and the Ark – And Tracking Aslan on the Move (Bible Talk, Ep. 21)" *Bible Talk* podcast, March 3, 2021, https://www.9marks.org/conversations/exodus-1-2-on-moses-and-the-ark-and-tracking-aslan-on-the-move-bible-talk-ep-21/, accessed October 22, 2021.

11. Jochebed

1. Mackay, J.L, ed., *Exodus: A Mentor Commentary* (Fearn, Ross-shire: Christian Focus Publications, 2001), 48.

12. Zipporah

1. Sproul, *Reformation Study Bible: ESV*, 100.
2. Moses was forty years old when he fled from Egypt (Acts 7:23) and returns when he was eighty (Ex. 7:7).
3. Alexander, T.D., and D.W. Baker, eds., *Dictionary of the Old Testament: Pentateuch* (Downers Grove, IL InterVarsity Press, 2003), 124.

13. Miriam

1. Mackay, J.L, *Exodus*, 48.
2. Alexander and Baker, *Dictionary of the OT: Pentateuch*, 569.
3. Moses married Zipporah, a Midianite, in Exodus 2:21 but his wife in Numbers 12:1 is called a Cushite. Habakkuk 3:7 equates Cushan with

Midian so perhaps Zipporah is in view here. However, most commentators believe that the repetition of "Cushite" in Numbers 12:1 implies a different woman, perhaps a second wife after the death of Zipporah.
4. "What is Hansen's Disease?" *Centers for Disease Control and Prevention*, February 10, 2017, https://www.cdc.gov/leprosy/about/about.html, accessed August 2, 2021.
5. Sproul, *Reformation Study Bible: ESV*, 217.

Part Four: Women of the Conquest and the Time of the Judges

14. Rahab

1. Sproul, *Everyone's a Theologian*, 238.

15. Deborah and Jael

1. Wolf, H., "Judges" in F.E. Gaebelein, ed., *The Expositor's Bible Commentary: Deuteronomy, Joshua, Judges, Ruth, 1,2 Samuel* (Grand Rapids, MI: Zondervan Publishing House, 1992), 404.
2. Wolf, "Judges," 406.
3. Wolf, "Judges," 407.

16. The Levite's Concubine

1. Sproul, *Everyone's a Theologian*, 384.
2. Wilson, M., "Is God a Misogynist?" *The Gospel Coalition*, audio, October 27, 2017, https://www.thegospelcoalition.org/conference_media/is-god-a-misogynist/, accessed August 2, 2021.

17. Naomi

1. Huey, F.B., Jr., "Ruth" in Gaebelein, *The Expositor's Bible Commentary: Deuteronomy to 2 Samuel*, 521–524.
2. Sproul, *Reformation Study Bible: ESV*, 398.

18. Ruth

1. Sproul, *Reformation Study Bible: ESV*, 396.

19. Hannah

1. Youngblood, R.F., "1, 2 Samuel" in Gaebelein, *The Expositor's Bible Commentary: Deuteronomy to 2 Samuel,* 571.
2. Youngblood, "1, 2 Samuel," 572.

Part Five: Women from Israel's Monarchy to the Exile

20. Abigail

1. Sproul, *Reformation Study Bible: ESV*, 440.

21. Bathsheba

1. Sproul, *Reformation Study Bible: ESV,* 463.
2. Youngblood, "1, 2 Samuel," 929.
3. Youngblood, "1, 2 Samuel," 929.

22. Tamar

1. Youngblood, "1, 2 Samuel," 956.
2. Youngblood, "1, 2 Samuel," 956.

23. Rizpah

1. Rizpah's son Mephibosheth in 2 Samuel 21:8 is not to be confused with Jonathan's son Mephibosheth in 2 Samuel 9:1–14.
2. Youngblood, "1, 2 Samuel," 1055.

24. The Widow of Zarephath

1. Sproul, *Reformation Study Bible: ESV*, 531.

25. Jezebel and Athaliah

1. Bunyan, J., *The Pilgrim's Progress*, (Leyland: Evangelical Press, 2017), 105–115.
2. MacArthur, *MacArthur Study Bible*, 498–9.
3. Newton, J., "Amazing Grace," hymn, 1779.

26. The Unfaithful Wife

1. Ryken and Ryken, *Literary Study Bible: ESV*, 1260.

27. Esther

1. The use of the name "Jew" for the people of Israel increases in parts of the Old Testament following the division of Israel into two kingdoms. The people of the southern kingdom of Judah (those exiled by the Babylonians, and thus the group in view in the book of Esther) became known as Jews.
2. Carswell, F., and S. Dargue, "Esther Rises (Chapter 2)," *Two Sisters and a Cup of Tea* podcast, October 1, 2021. https://twosistersandacupoftea.buzzsprout.com/1546822/9162073-esther-rises-chapter-2, accessed October 2, 2021.
3. Sproul, *Reformation Study Bible: ESV*, 736.

Part Six: Women between the Testaments to Christ

28. Elizabeth

1. Sproul, *Reformation Study Bible: ESV*, 1659
2. Sproul, *Reformation Study Bible: ESV*, 1781.
3. Vinson, R.B., *Luke: Smyth and Helwys Bible Commentary* (Macon, GA: Smyth and Helwys Publishing, Inc., 2008), 29.

29. Mary

1. MacArthur, *MacArthur Study Bible*, 498–9.
2. MacArthur, *MacArthur Study Bible*, 1537.
3. Kreitzer, B. et al., eds. *Luke: New Testament*, Vol. III (Downers Grove, IL: IVP Academic., 2015), 15.
4. Sproul, *Reformation Study Bible: ESV*, 1782.
5. Sproul, *Reformation Study Bible: ESV*, 1783.

30. Christ, the Seed of the Woman

1. DeYoung, K., "Our Pro-Woman, Complementarian Jesus?" *The Gospel Coalition*, February 15, 2016, https://www.thegospelcoalition.org/article/our-pro-woman-complementarian-jesus/, accessed October 13, 2021.

Acknowledgments

I've had the dream of writing a book about women in the Bible and Christ for decades. Eric Dolce was the first person to hear my hopes for this project. He prayed for me, supported the idea, and never doubted that this day would come. Eric, thank you for being my greatest encouragement.

Jael and Noel, I appreciate your endless prayers for mommy throughout the writing process. You are gifts! May you grow into women whose lives point to Jesus, may he be the center of your certain hope. Anthony, you joined our family as a tiny infant days before the start of this project. I call you my "coauthor" because you were often in my arms as I wrote. Like the disciples of the Emmaus Road, may you be taught by the risen Christ and may your heart burn with affection for him.

Dear Robert Kinney, your willingness to give eyes and thoughts to this project, amid a very busy schedule, will always be remembered. Thank you! To my sisters, Sike Osinuga, Sasha McGee, Emily Halle, and Juana Hawkins, I am grateful for your precious time and prayerful feedback. You shaped my writing for the better.

Many women supported and prayed for me throughout the publishing process: Andrea Whyte, Bora Jin, Laura Thomas, Colleen McFadden, Hope Abdelrahman, Plina Doyle, and Phyllis Anderson, thank you for being such good friends to me. To the ladies of Tea and Theology small group, you were my first students on this topic. Thanks for being a part of the journey.

To the 10ofThose family, I'm grateful for the honor of working with you to point others to Jesus! And above all, I thank the King whose kindness to me cannot be measured (Eph. 2:7).

Scripture Index

Genesis

Exodus

Leviticus

Numbers

Deuteronomy

Joshua

1 Kings

2 Kings

1 Chronicles

2 Chronicles

Ezra

Esther

Job

Psalms

Proverbs

Isaiah

Jeremiah

Ezekiel

Hosea

Micah

Malachi

Matthew

Mark

Luke

John